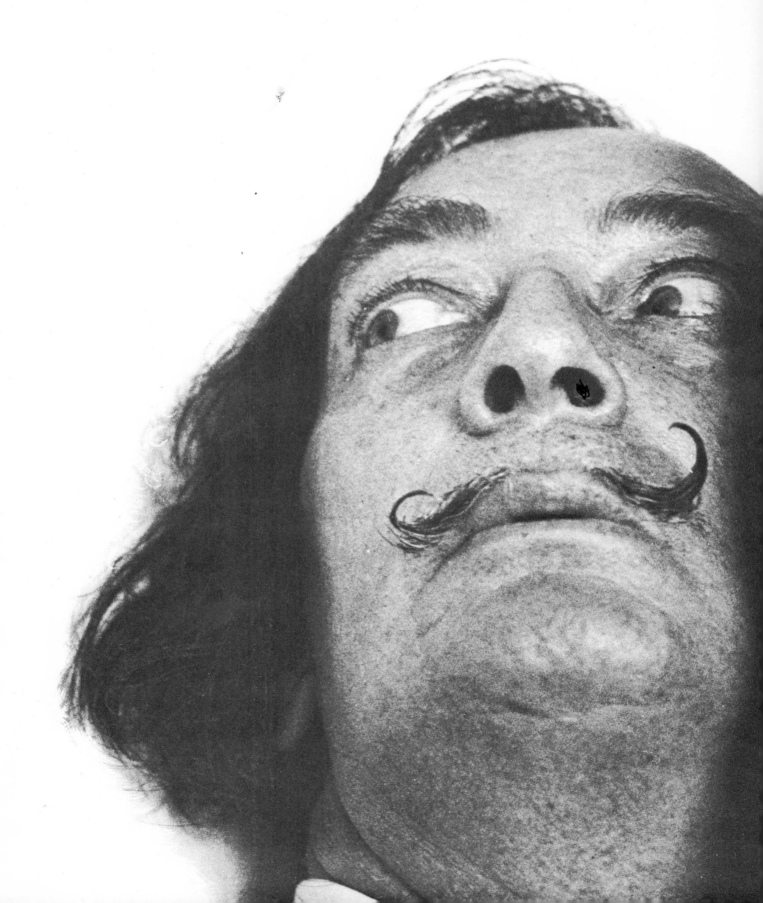

dali

dali

conroy maddox

crown publishers inc
new york

The author and publishers would like to thank Salvador Dali and
Enrique Sabater for their kind co-operation in preparing this book.

N
7113
D3
M32

4/80   9.09   Campbell

Title spread left: The Dali Museum, at Figueras, Spain.

© Copyright The Hamlyn Publishing Group Limited 1979
London · New York · Sydney · Toronto
Astronaut House, Feltham, Middlesex, England

Maddox, Conroy.
    Dali.
    1. Dali, Salvador, 1904 —   2. Artists — Spain —
Biography.   I. Title
N7113.D3M32   759.6 (B)   78-9924
ISBN 0-517-53675-7

First published 1979 in the United States of America by
Crown Publishers, Inc., New York.

Phototypeset in England by Filmtype Services Limited, Scarborough.
Printed in Hong Kong.

contents

Plate 1 **The Burning Giraffe**

6

introduction

Whatever the future judgement of Salvador Dali may be, it cannot be denied that he has a place all his own in the history of modern art. His fame has been an issue of controversy, kept alive as much by Dali's own provocative exhibitionism as by the critics and press, who have so consistently condemned him for his excesses: 'neurotic', 'egocentric' and 'mad' are words not infrequently used when referring to him. Over the years he has become so closely identified with Surrealism that it is possible to say that in the public mind Surrealism simply is Salvador Dali. Considering the publicity there is some excuse for this prevailing error.

Whatever his influence has been on the art of the 20th century, few can deny the validity of his contribution. In fact, it could be argued that it is as great as that of his famous fellow-countryman, Picasso. Dali himself has said: 'Picasso is less of a painter, but he is the most destructive genius of modern times.' Certainly the revelatory nature of Dali's imagery between 1929 and 1939 was the most potent of our age, which makes it that much more difficult to assess its aesthetic worth. From early childhood he was abnormally imaginative, selfishly preoccupied with his own pleasures, cynically parading his audacity and his perverse violence, the intimate details of which he did not hesitate to boast of in his memoirs. In his book *Surrealism* Julien Levy sees him as 'a man who bears the stigma of the Spanish Inquisition, the sexual ecstasies of Spain's mystics . . .' and we have only to explore the iconography of his work to affirm the connection with that Spanish heritage.

If the problem is correctly stated, then Dali, though not alone in the field (the Surrealist Manifesto was launched in 1924, some five years before Dali's involvement), is perhaps the first to have consistently exploited the findings of Freud and psychoanalysis and to have deliberately insisted on the rights of man to his own madness. His development of a 'paranoiac-critical' approach, which he brought to bear so excessively into all aspects of thought, was one of the most revolutionary contributions to Surrealism and was the touchstone which gave Dali's work its unique character and dominated his evolution as an artist. To follow his development is to follow the

Plate 1
The Burning Giraffe
1935
Oil on canvas
$10\frac{5}{8} \times 13\frac{3}{4}$ in (27 × 35 cm)
Kunstmuseum, Basel

By 1934, Dali's use of what he called 'handmade photography', with its sharply defined colour areas, had given way to a more aesthetic use of colour as well as a lyricism in his handling of form.

Plate 2
Beach Scene with Telephone
1938
Oil on canvas
29 × 36¼ in (73 × 92 cm)
Edward James Foundation

Dali's interest in the telephone dates from the Munich crisis of 1938 that preceded the Second World War.

fertile imagination and manual dexterity that he was to bring to Surrealism at a particular time. As early as 1920 André Breton, who was to play such an important part in the Surrealist movement, had proposed 'allegiance to folly, to dreams, to the incoherent, to the hyperbolic – in a word to all that is contrary to the general appearance of reality'. Several years would go by before Dali was to make his pictorial and critical participation; it is necessary, therefore, that we trace his development and the influences that were to have such a crucial effect on what he was to call his images of 'concrete irrationality'.

8

biography

Salvador Dali was born at eight forty-five on the morning of 11th May 1904, in the Spanish town of Figueras, where his father was a notary and man of some local importance. The name Salvador had originally been given to his brother who had died three years before Dali was born. An only child until his sister Ana María arrived, he was thoroughly spoilt and allowed to do almost anything he pleased. In his autobiography, Dali gives a vivid account of these early years: 'My brother and I resembled each other like two drops of water, but we had different reflections. Like myself he had the unmistakeable facial morphology of a genius. He gave signs of alarming precocity, but his glance was veiled by a melancholy, characterising insurmountable intelligence. I, on the other hand, was much less intelligent but I reflected everything. I was to become the prototype *par excellence* of the phenomenally retarded "polymorphous perverse" having kept intact all the reminiscences of the nursling's erogenic paradises; I clutched at pleasure with boundless, selfish eagerness and on the slightest provocation I would become dangerous.'[1] He does not neglect to record other memories, such as his intra-uterine life 'as though it were yesterday'; he identifies it as paradise, and also the colour of hell, but soft, warm and immobile. One of his pre-birth visions, he tells us, was that of a pair of eggs fried in a pan – but without the pan – 'an ever-hallucinatory image' which he could later reproduce at will, a phosphene.[2]

His education began in a local school and then in the Academy in Figueras, run by the Brothers of the Marist Order. It was a period of little learning, and his school reports were received by his parents with consternation. A desire to do the exact opposite of what everyone else did assumed immense importance in his eyes, and hours were spent dreaming up the most anti-social acts in order to astonish his schoolmates. Many revealed themselves in acts of aggression. Walking with a young boy one day, he pushed him over a bridge on to the rocks some fifteen feet below, and then spent the afternoon eating cherries in a rocking chair as he watched the blood-stained basins being brought from the bedroom. Alone with his three-year-old sister, he dealt her a terrible kick on the head, which gave him a

[1] From *The Secret Life of Salvador Dali*, by Salvador Dali, translated by Haakon M. Chevalier, new enlarged edition 1961, copyright © 1946, 1961 by Salvador Dali, used with permission of the Dial Press. British and Commonwealth edition Vision Press, London.

[2] A sensation that results from pressure on the closed eyes.

9

Plate 3
Satirical drawing
1920
Ink on cardboard
Collection Enrique Sabater

One of Dali's earliest known works, this cartoon was done as a present for his uncle.

[1] *The Case of Salvador Dali.*

'delirious joy'. He was given a wounded bat one day and took it to his hiding place in a wash-house. Next morning it lay, half dead, covered with frenzied ants. Overcome with emotion, he bit into the writhing mass. He also found an inexplicable pleasure in throwing himself down steps. The pain was insignificant, the intense joy was overwhelming, and he was encouraged to repeat the performance many times, not unaware of the effect it produced on his fellow pupils. On another occasion he smashed a boy's violin to prove that painting was superior to music.

Before Dali was six years old, he was showing considerable talent as an artist. Fleur Cowles in her book[1] on Dali reproduces the earliest known work, a landscape painted postcard-size. It was followed by two much more ambitious works, *Portrait of Helen of Troy* and *Joseph Greeting his Brethren*, executed in the precise 19th-century literary style. For a studio, Dali was given the use of an old wash-house at the top of the house. On hot days he would fill a tub full of water, remove his clothes and sit in it for hours, painting. Pinned to the walls around were his paintings, carried out on the covers of hat boxes taken from his aunt's millinery shop, as well as reproductions of the Renaissance masters torn from magazines. Here he found refuge, and the solitude that he always so desperately sought. To be alone became a mania, and all kinds of excuses were found which would permit him to rush upstairs to the laundry. Here he felt unique, living out his fantasies, playing at being a genius: 'if you play at genius, you become one.'

Still subject to heights of delirious egocentricity, his parents, not unaware of his growing artistic ability, sent him to a friend of theirs in the country. Ramón Pitchot was a rich connoisseur of art and a gifted painter in the Impressionist manner. It was a considerably talented family. Two sons were musicians, one of the daughters was an opera singer and another was married to a Spanish poet. Their estate was known as the Muli de la Torre (The Tower Mill). Dali's period with this family was to have an important influence on his life and illuminates many of the erotic fantasies that were to appear in later works.

Although the practical side of the mill had little interest, the tower produced a powerful effect on his imagination. It became a 'sacred spot', the very centre of his world. Each day he would have his meals in a room hung with the many Impressionist paintings of Ramón Pitchot. To the young Dali these 'visual cocktails' with their brilliant decorative unity were an endless fascination. It was not long before he was deeply committed to this new and exciting way of looking at nature. 'It represented,' he tells us, 'my first contact with an anti-academic and revolutionary aesthetic theory.'

Pitchot provided him with a large whitewashed room as a studio where, consumed by a creative fever, he explored the instantaneous luminosity that he found so tantalising in these new paintings. On one occasion, having used up all his canvas, he decided to utilise an old wooden door, somewhat worm-eaten, for a subject that had been in his mind for some time, a still-life of a large bunch of cherries. They were to be painted in three colours only and applied directly from the tube. Setting up an immense pile of cherries as a model, he attacked the wooden surface. Soon he found that he was painting to the rhythm of the mill, each cherry being realised with three touches of colour – vermilion for the lighter side, carmine for the shade, white for the highlight. The whole effect, with the thick daubs of colour, assumed an astonishing realism. Completely engrossed in keeping up with the sound of the mill, he discovered that he had forgotten to add the stems. 'Suddenly, I had an idea. I took a handful of cherries and began to eat them. As soon as one of them was swallowed, I would glue the stem directly to my painting in the appropriate place.' The gluing on of cherry stems produced an unforeseen effect of startling 'finish'. To further reinforce the realism, he then proceeded to introduce real worms into the wormholes, which looked as though they belonged to the painted cherries. It must have been an impressive work. Pitchot, who turned up at that moment, was heard to mutter, 'That shows genius.'

His time at the Tower Mill fell into a ritual. Waking in the morning he went through an exhibitionist fantasy with the maid. At breakfast,

Plate 4
Cadaqués
1923
Oil on canvas
38 × 50 in (96.5 × 127 cm)
Private collection

Cadaqués is a small fishing village where Dali spent his summers while still a student.

because he liked the sensation, he poured hot milk and coffee down his chest, then went to the studio to paint. Here, he tell us, he worked on 'pictorial inventions, re-invention of Impressionism, reaffirmation and rebirth of my aesthetic megalomania'.

Before Dali was to leave the Pitchots' there was a notable incident dominated by an object that was to find its way into his gallery of recurrent images. At the time of the linden blossom picking, helping to fetch the ladders from the tower attic, he discovered a heavy metal crown, used for some theatrical production, and an old crutch. It was an exciting find, loaded with fetishistic significance. Among the blossom pickers was an extremely attractive woman with large and turgescent breasts, accompanied by her twelve-year-old daughter. Dali instantly fell in love with the child, identifying her with all his false memories of the ideal woman. Finding his impulsive behaviour only succeeded in frightening the young girl, he found solace in

Plate 5
Apparatus and Hand
1927
Oil on panel
$24\frac{1}{2} \times 18\frac{3}{4}$ in (62 × 47.5 cm)
Private collection

Between 1925 and 1928, Dali rejected his abstract experiments to come under the influence of Picasso and the Cubist movement. Nevertheless, he had not lost touch with his early training based on the realist tradition and continued to produce representational works of considerable technical precision. This work is beginning to show evidence of his growing hallucinatory power.

covertly watching the mother, in particular her large firm breasts, beneath which he had a voluptuous desire to rest the upper bifurcated part of the newly discovered crutch. Overcome with longing, he invented a ruse which could fulfil the fantasy. Finding a closed area lit only by a small window overlooking the garden, his attention was drawn to three melons hanging from the rafters. They suggested to his feverish mind a substitute even more desirable than the woman's breasts. Carefully entangling his diabolo in the vines that grew on the outside wall above the window, he then asked the blossom picker to retrieve the toy. While she moved the ladder to the desired spot, he rushed back to the room, stripped off his clothes, placed the crown on his head and covered himself with an ermine cloak. At the exact moment the upper part of the woman's body filled the small window space, he let slip the cloak from his naked body and gently placed the crutch beneath the lower part of one of the ripening melons, pressing it into the soft fruit, at the same time staring back and forth between the swollen breasts and the melon. Under the persistent pressure, the melon began to drip, covering him with its sweet and sticky juice. Further pressure detached the melon, which fell on to his head at the exact moment the woman, having disentangled the diabolo, descended the ladder. Hurriedly throwing himself on the floor he lay breathless, waiting, unsuccessfully, to be discovered. Trembling with exhaustion, the two remaining melons appeared as a 'sinister symbol and no longer evoked the beautiful blossom-gatherer's two breasts, sunny with afternoon. Instead, they too now seemed to stir like two dead things rolled into balls, like two petrified hedgehogs.'

The secret pleasure Dali derived from that crutch has remained with him ever since, not only as a fetish in erotic acts, but as a predominant image in many obsessive and fanciful ways in his paintings. Later he was to conceive the idea of a tiny facial crutch to be worn by 'criminally elegant women', so that they could experience 'the sacred tug of their exhibitionism encrusted in the flesh of their own faces'.

Encouraged by Pitchot, Dali's father enrolled him in Señor Nuñez's art classes in Figueras. Nuñez appears to have been a sympathetic teacher. Perhaps he sensed something of the later brilliance in his eccentric but dedicated pupil. Stimulated by the individual attention he received, Dali was soon reviving his passion for the great masters of the Renaissance and exploring the mysteries of chiaroscuro. Reading also began to be an obsession, with philosophy as his favourite subject. Nietzsche's *Thus Spake Zarathustra* and Voltaire's *Philosophical Dictionary* became firm favourites. His real joy was Kant, whom he read and re-read without understanding a word: 'such an important and useless book'. He dipped into Spinoza, and then Descartes on whom he was to base many of his later researches. His paintings were now beginning to attract attention, and invitations to show in local and regional exhibitions followed.

In the meanwhile, secondary studies continued at the Marist School, although most of the teachers had given up any hope of

Plate 6 **The Lugubrious Game**

Plate 6
The Lugubrious Game
1929
Oil and collage on canvas
12¾ × 16⅛ in (31 × 41 cm)
Claude Hersaint Collection, Paris

The first truly Surrealist painting by Dali. The scatological elements were of some concern to the Surrealists when they first saw this work.

Plate 7
The First Days of Spring
1929
Oil on board with collage
19¾ × 25⅝ in (50 × 65 cm)
Private collection

Dali's working method during this period was to adapt the Surrealist processes of automatic writing to painting, of trying to see 'like a medium' the images that would appear in his imagination.

Plate 8 **Accommodations of Desire**

Plate 9 **Illumined Pleasures**

teaching him anything. Nose-bleeding and 'angina' became regular means of avoiding the hateful lessons. Frantically he awaited vacation time, which was always spent in the village of Cadaqués on the Mediterranean coast. The rocks and beaches which he came to know so well in his solitary wanderings became the very spot which he adored with a 'fanatical fidelity' and which he thought the most beautiful landscape in the world, with rocky contours that only Leonardo could have captured. It was to affect his vision profoundly: those strangely coloured rocks and deserted beaches are faithfully imprinted and appear in many studies with extraordinary love and clarity. Dali made the geological phenomena of Catalonia very much his own.

Although the family had little faith in his earning a living by art, they realised the futility of trying to convince their young son. A compromise was proposed, that he should attend the School of Fine Art in Madrid, qualify as a professor and use his free time to paint as he liked. Dali agreed with enthusiasm. He had been working hard and won two prizes. He was seventeen years of age and supremely confident of his ability. Suddenly Figueras was stifling, and Madrid offered independence, an escape from the watchful eyes of his family. Admission to the School of Fine Arts was dependent on an examination, a drawing of a classical subject made to exact measurements. According to Dali's account, he chose to ignore the instructions completely, making the drawing too small. Re-drawing, he made it too large. On the final day of submission, panic-stricken, he made another attempt, this time even smaller than the first. Nevertheless, so perfect was the study that he was accepted as a student.

For months he behaved as a model pupil. All social life was shunned. Sundays were spent at the Prado making Cubist sketches of the various paintings. He had just discovered one of the Cubist masters, Juan Gris, and was in full revolt against Impressionism. The rainbow palette was replaced with black, white, sienna and olive green. If the colours were sombre, the same could not be said of his attire. Long trousers were discarded in favour of short pants with stockings, sometimes puttees, a long waterproof cape, hair sticking out like a mane beneath a large black felt hat, and an unlit pipe clenched between his teeth. Whatever enthusiasm he had for the teaching ability at the Academy in the early months soon gave way to disappointment. He felt they had nothing to offer. To his searching questions about art, they had only evasive answers, such as: 'It's temperament that counts – no rules, no constraints. Simplify.' 'I was expecting to find limits, rigour, science,' he remarked, 'I was offered liberty, laziness, approximations.' Yet he continued to be an exemplary student, never missing a class and always respectful. The professors found him cold, too cerebral, but clever and always successful with his work.

His growing frustration with the Academy is amusingly highlighted by the incident of the plaster. One day, entering the sculpture room during the lunch period, he emptied sacks of plaster into a basin

Plate 8
Accommodations of Desire
1929
Oil on panel
$8\frac{5}{8} \times 13\frac{3}{4}$ in (22 × 35 cm)
Mr and Mrs Julien Levy Collection, New York

Desire, for Dali, is expressed through the 'terrorising images of lions' heads'.

Plate 9
Illumined Pleasures
1929
Oil and collage on composition board
$9\frac{3}{8} \times 13\frac{3}{4}$ in (23.8 × 35 cm)
The Sidney and Harriet Janis Collection, Gift to the Museum of Modern Art, New York

Although part of this picture is composed of collage, the skilfully painted areas create confusion about what is paint and what is photography. Dali's debt to de Chirico is revealed in the picture within the picture as well as in the emotive use of perspective. Other influences derive from Max Ernst (the bird totem on the left of the centre box) and Magritte (the painted cyclists on the right). In a number of early works, he pasted down line engravings and photographs which were then faithfully copied so as to be indistinguishable from the original, as in another painting, *Accommodations of Desire* of 1929 (plate 8).

Plate 10
The Hand: Remorse
1930
Oil on canvas
16¼ × 26 in (41.3 × 66 cm)
Private collection

The architecture and ornamentation of Art Nouveau with its 'undulant-convulsive' style is evident in this painting. The head of the girl behind the seated figure suggests that it was a direct copy from a work in the 'Modern Style'.

under the running tap. Soon the floor was inundated with the milk-white liquid which spread under the door and cascaded with catastrophic force down the stairway to spill out into the entrance hall. Thoroughly frightened by the magnitude of his action, he ploughed through the avalanche to the exit, but not before stopping to admire the fast-hardening mass.

It was about this time that he discovered Freud. *The Interpretation of Dreams* was of major importance in his life. The most casual act was subjected to agonising self-analysis, and he was to go through tortures trying to decide whether he was really mad. His dreams, he found, were always linked to an actual event, ending in the exact spot and the same situation in which he found himself upon awakening.

The artistic and literary developments in Europe, particularly Dadaism, with its mockery of all accepted values and sensational outbursts of exhibitionism, had not passed unnoticed among some of the students at the Academy. Luis Buñuel, García Lorca, Pedro Garfias and Eugenio Montes were the moving spirits of this small but wild band in which Dali was soon to occupy a position of importance. They praised his Cubist paintings, listened excitedly to his extravagant ideas. It was not long, he assures us, before it was 'Dali this, Dali that and Dali everything'. It was all very exciting. He became an habitué of the cafes, joining in the noisy intellectual discussions on art and literature, women and sex. The outlandish clothes were discarded for expensive suits and silk shirts, the pallid face was streaked with make-up, and he took to plastering his hair down with picture varnish.

An act of rebellion in support of one of the teachers brought about his temporary suspension from the Academy for a year. He returned to his worried father in Figueras, where shortly afterwards he was arrested by the Civil Guard and spent a month in prison. Considerable revolutionary agitation was taking place at the time, and Dali, with his wild talk of anarchy and monarchy, was immediately suspect. Since no charges could be found on which to try him, he was finally set free.

Again he left for Cadaqués, where he became an 'ascetic once more and where I literally gave myself over body and soul to painting and to my philosophic research'. He knew that once he returned to Madrid he would soon revert to the old ways. But in the meantime it was to be all discipline and work. 'I was in fact a monster,' he said, 'whose anatomical parts were an eye, a hand and a brain.'

At the end of the disciplinary period he returned to the Academy and immediately established his reputation for irreverence and rebellion. Given as a painting subject a Gothic statue of the Virgin, he chose to paint a pair of scales. 'Perhaps you see a virgin like everyone else,' he told the astonished teacher, 'I see a pair of scales.' There is little doubt that at this time Dali was going through several opposing experiments in painting. He explored the problems of Italian Futurism, particularly their attempts to suggest objects in motion. From 1924 the interest shifted to the Scuola Metafisica (the

Plate 10 **The Hand : Remorse**

Plate 11
Shades of Night Descending
1931
Oil on canvas
24 × 19¾ in (61 × 50 cm)
Collection of Mr and Mrs
A. Reynolds Morse, Salvador Dali
Museum, Cleveland (Ohio)

The geology of the Catalan coast.
Dali has refused to look at any other
landscape.

Metaphysical School), a movement evolved by Giorgio de Chirico
and Carlo Carrà. De Chirico had had his art training in Munich, where
he had come under the influence of the Swiss-German, Arnold
Böcklin, with all his mysticism and romanticism. Nietzsche's writing
on *Symbolical dream pictures* and Schopenhauer's *Essay on Apparitions* were to contribute to his enigmatic and disquieting dream
imagery. The mystery of his city streets and deserted squares, with
their own laws of perspective and veiled childhood memories, are
some of the most poetic statements of our age. They proposed a
rejection of Cubism and Futurism, affirming in their place an art of
the metaphysical, a return to dreams and inner perception. In Paris
the Surrealists had not failed to recognise the extreme originality of
what de Chirico had achieved.

For Dali, it was to bring him that step nearer the means of external-
ising his obsessions. It was all the more surprising, therefore, in view
of his later development in Surrealism and his vehement rejection of
abstraction, that he should suddenly turn back to the Cubism of
Picasso. James Thrall Soby puts forward the theory that 'Dali had

inevitably to face the issue which Cubism had raised in European art. Reduced to a dramatic decision, this issue consisted in whether a given younger artist should be for or against Picasso's dictates', and he goes on to say: 'Remembering that Picasso was a fellow Catalan, one can understand why Dali should have been caught, at some point, by the immense suction of his ideas.' Yet it is not inconceivable that Dali sensed in the classical structure and abstracted subject-matter of Cubism a security that, at least for a time, would provide some steadying control over the disordered nature of his innermost thoughts, which were now beginning to possess him, thoughts that were no longer to lead a merely subjectively delusional existence, but were to be made objectively perceptible in painting. It is no accident that, after his rejection of Cubism, he should have painted *The Lugubrious Game* (plate 6), with its provocative scatology and in particular its coprophagic element.

Committing himself to Cubism, Dali undertook a visit to Paris in 1927 to see Picasso. According to Dali's account, he arrived deeply moved and full of respect. 'I have come to see you before visiting the Louvre,' he told the artist. 'You're quite right,' replied Picasso. Dali then showed him a small painting he had brought, which Picasso studied without comment. For the next two hours he contemplated the canvases that Picasso dragged from the studio, also without any comment. On his leaving, they exchanged glances which meant, Dali assures us, 'You get the idea?' 'I get it.'

Another account of this visit speaks of Dali taking a tape measure with him and in complete silence proceeding to measure the size of each canvas placed before him.

After his return to Figueras, Luis Buñuel proposed collaboration on a film which his mother was prepared to finance. Dali found the

Plate 12
L'Age d'Or
The Golden Age
1931

After *Un Chien Andalou* in 1929, Dali and Buñuel collaborated on a second Surrealist film financed by the Vicomte de Noailles in 1931. Dali's scenario called for archbishops with embroidered tiaras bathing among the rocks of Cape Creus. He also suggested a few 'blasphematory scenes' which were to be presented with fanaticism in order to 'achieve the grandeur of a true and authentic sacrilege'.

21

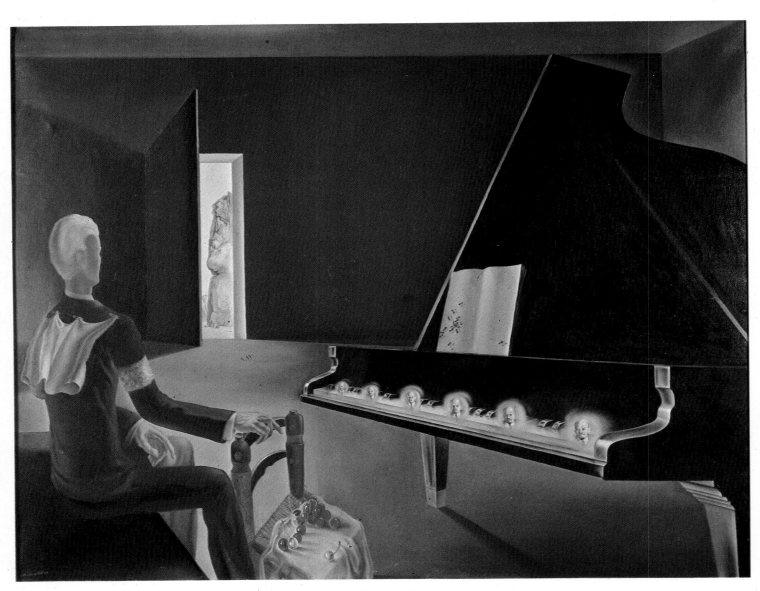

Plate 13 **Six Apparitions of Lenin on a Piano**

script naive and mediocre, and suggested in its place a scenario he had just completed. Its theme was of 'adolescence and death'. Together they worked on the plot, and also the title–it was to be called *Un Chien Andalou*. Buñuel hurried back to Paris to undertake the production, while Dali stayed behind to 'sharpen all my doctrinal means at a distance'.

His one-man exhibition at the Dalmau Gallery in Barcelona had been seen by Picasso during a brief visit to that city. Back in Paris he had spoken enthusiastically about the show to his dealer, Paul Rosenberg, who wrote asking for photographs, which Dali neglected to send. 'I knew,' he said, 'that the day I arrived in Paris, I would put them all in my bag with one sweep.' Another Spanish painter, Joan Miró, wrote and followed this up with a visit to Figueras with his gallery director, Pierre Loeb. For all Miró's generous support, Loeb remained sceptical, finding Dali's painting too confusing and lacking in personality. Dali must have found it a disappointment. Paris was where the battle was being fought and he intended, somehow, to participate in it. His exhibitions in Barcelona and Madrid had been highly successful, the reviews flattering. The magazine *d'Aci, d'Alla* had written: 'we are absolutely certain that if the young artist does not wander away, he will be one of those who will give the greatest glory to Catalan painting in our century ...' *La Publicidad* could not find among the young painters a more fascinating figure than that of this young man from Figueras. With the attention he was also getting from Paris, the very centre of the art world, his father was finally convinced that he should go.

The year was 1928 when Dali arrived in Paris. He was not thinking of another visit to Picasso, but, as he tells us, he turned to the taxi driver and asked, 'Do you know any good whorehouses?' 'Get in, Monsieur,' he answered, with somewhat wounded pride, though in a fatherly way. 'Don't worry, I know them all.'

He visited the 'Chabanais' which must have impressed him, for some twelve years later, speaking of the three spots that produced in him the deepest sense of mystery, he cited the stairway of the 'Chabanais' for its ugly eroticism, the Theatre of Palladio in Vicenza, the divine aesthetic, and the entrance to the tombs of the Kings of the Escorial as the 'most mysterious and beautiful mortuary spot'.

Miró did not desert his young friend and was full of advice on how to go about making the right connections in Paris society. First, he must get a dinner-jacket. He must not talk too much and go in for some physical culture. Tomorrow he would meet Tristan Tzara, the Dadaist leader. The social rounds continued – the Duchesse de Dato, the Comtesse Cuevas de Vera, Goemans, who was to become his dealer, Pavlik Tchelitchev, Robert Desnos, who wanted to buy his painting *The First Days of Spring* (plate 7). Pierre Loeb, who still hoped one day to show him, took him to the Bal Tabarin, where he met that 'legendary being,' Paul Eluard, the Surrealist poet. He looked in on Buñuel. *Un Chien Andalou* was going into production, and he helped with some of the effects. The requirements were

Plate 13
Six Apparitions of Lenin on a Piano
1931 or 1933
Oil on canvas
$57\frac{3}{8} \times 44\frac{7}{8}$ in (146×114 cm)
Musée National d'Art Moderne, Paris

Although Dali refused to associate himself with the revolutionary aspects of Surrealism, this painting was inspired by the leader of the Russian revolution. A less charitable portrayal of Lenin is to be seen in the painting *The Enigma of William Tell* (plate 23) painted in 1934.

Plate 14
The Persistence of Memory
1931
Oil on canvas
$9\frac{1}{2} \times 13$ in (24.2 × 33 cm)
Museum of Modern Art, New York

Dali has said that eating Camembert cheese inspired the limp watches: 'Be persuaded that Salvador Dali's famous limp watches are nothing else than the tender, extravagant and solitary paranoiac-critical Camembert of time and space.' This image was to make its appearance in many subsequent works.

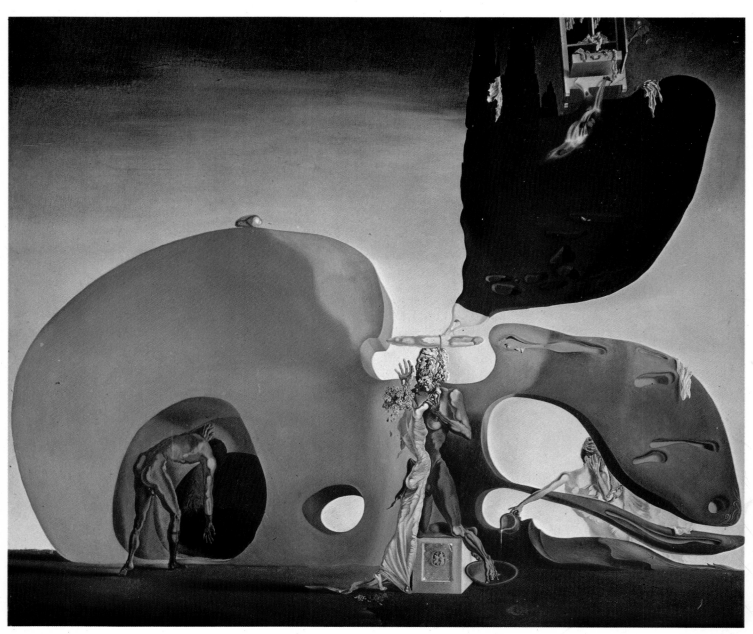

Plate 15 **The Birth of Liquid Desires**

formidable – a nude model who was to have live sea-urchins under each arm, several decomposed donkeys, a grand piano, a cut-off hand, three ants' nests and a cow's eye.

The winter of 1929 saw the first showing of *Un Chien Andalou*. Praised by the Surrealists for its dream sequences and arresting imagery, the audience had little stomach for a film that opened with a woman's eye being sliced by a razor in close-up. The following year saw their second film *L'Age d'Or* (*The Golden Age*) (plate 12), financed by the Vicomte de Noailles. Full of violence and revolt, it showed archbishops and bones among the rocks of Cape Creus, a blind man being ill-treated, a dog crushed to death, a son killed by his father, and a character from de Sade disguised as Christ. Riots broke out, with the right-wing pro-Hitler group, the 'Camelots du Roy', smashing up the cinema. The police intervened and further showings were banned.[1]

For all Dali's frenetic activity, the success which he so desperately sought did not come. It was an intolerable situation. Shunning his new-found friends to spend hours sitting in cafés or wandering the boulevards, he felt again the touch of madness. The following evening 'I thus hung my illness on the coathanger of the Gare d'Orsay ...' He caught a train for Spain.

Back in Cadaqués the recent events disappeared, replaced with the wonders and fantasies of childhood. Strange images, he tells us, took possession of his mind, rising enigmatically from out of the dark. The immediate thought was to make a painting to reproduce each image in all its clarity and as scrupulously as possible. It would be completely automatic, without conscious intervention, obeying only his authentic, biological desire. *The Lugubrious Game* (plate 6) – the title was suggested by Eluard – was Dali's first truly Surrealist painting. In his autobiography he wrote:

'This work, unusual and disconcerting in the highest degree, was by the very physiology of its elaboration far removed from the "Dadaist collage", which is always a poetic and *a posteriori* arrangement. It was also the contrary of Chirico's metaphysical painting, for here the spectator had perforce to believe in the earthy reality of the subject, which was one of an elementary and frenzied biological nature. And it was furthermore the contrary of the poetic softening of certain abstract paintings which continue stupidly, like blind moths, to bump into the extinguished lamps of the neo-Platonic light.

'I, then, and only I was the true Surrealist painter, at least according to the definition which its chief, André Breton, gave of Surrealism. Nevertheless, when Breton saw this painting, he hesitated for a long time before its scatological elements, for in the picture appeared a figure seen from behind, whose drawers were bespattered with excrement. The involuntary aspect of this element, so characteristic in psychopathological iconography, should have sufficed to enlighten him. But I was obliged to justify myself by saying that it was merely a simulacrum. No further questions were asked. But had I been

Plate 15
The Birth of Liquid Desires
1932
Oil on canvas
$44\frac{1}{4} \times 37\frac{1}{2}$ in (112 × 95 cm)
Peggy Guggenheim Collection, Venice

[1] For a detailed account of *Un Chien Andalou* and *L'Age d'Or* see J. H. Matthews, *Surrealism and Film*, The University of Michigan Press, Ann Arbor, 1971.

Plate 16 **Fried Eggs without the Plate**

28

Plate 16
Fried Eggs without the Plate
Oeufs sur le Plat sans le Plat
1932
Oil on canvas
23¾ × 16½ in (60.4 × 42 cm)
Collection of Mr and Mrs
A. Reynolds Morse, Salvador Dali
Museum, Cleveland (Ohio)

The pun in the original French title
is untranslatable into English.

Plate 17
**Ordinary French Bread with
Two Fried Eggs, without a
Plate, on Horseback, Trying to
Sodomise a Crumb of
Portuguese Bread**
1932
Oil on wood
6¼ × 12⅝ in (16.8 × 32 cm)
Takahashi Shoji collection, Tokyo

The image of fried eggs was an
'ever-hallucinatory image' for Dali,
which he claimed to be able to
produce at will by putting pressure
on his closed eyes. Eggs appeared
in a number of works around this
period, including *Fried Eggs without
the Plate* (plate 16).

pressed, I should certainly have had to answer that it was the simulacrum of the excrement itself. This idealistic narrowness was, from my point of view, the fundamental "intellectual vice" of the early period of Surrealism. Hierarchies were established where there was no need for any. Between the excrement and a piece of rock crystal, by the very fact that they both sprang from the common basis of the unconscious, there could and should be no difference in category. And these were the men who denied the hierarchies of tradition!'[1]

During this period in Cadaqués, there was to be a deepening of his visionary imagination, an inextinguishable fecundity of experiments and an enrichment of his technique. His sympathies were now wholeheartedly with the Surrealists. The summer of 1929 saw not only *The Lugubrious Game* but also *Accommodations of Desire* (plate 8) in which he turned to collage, the pasting of photographic or engraved elements on to his canvas. He used this not as Picasso and the Cubists had done, as a formal means and an extension of the painter's palette,

Plate 18
Memory of the Child-Woman
1932
Oil on canvas
39 × 47¼ in (99 × 110 cm)
Private collection

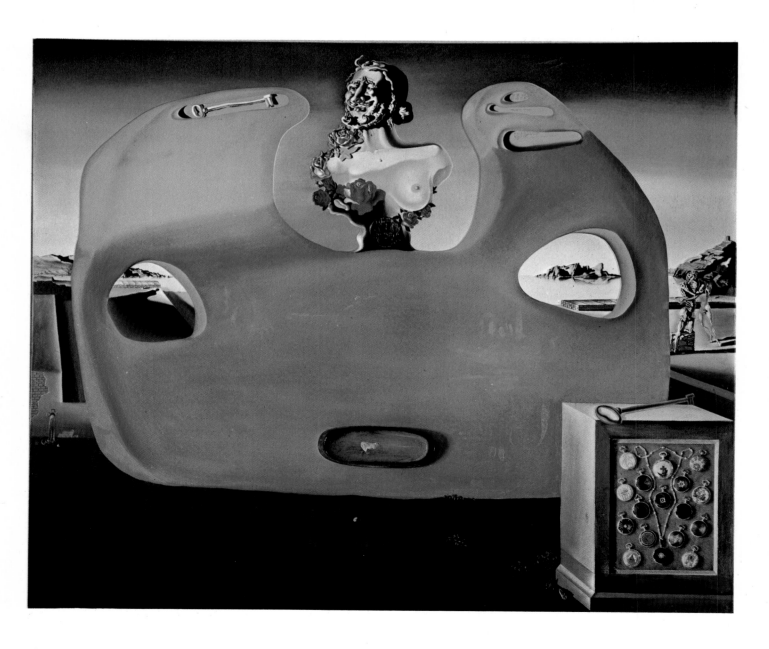

integrating the painted cuttings with the brushwork in a purely textural way. Instead he exploited the disruptive potential of collage. Rather than playing down the subject matter, he used it to dramatise the psychological and social objectives, with its pictorial aspect always used as a vehicle for the communication of ideas. Although the head of the lion is a photographic cut-out, the overall exactitude of the printed areas in the work is so perfect that we are confused by what is collage and what is paint.

Of the same year is *Illumined Pleasures* (plate 9) which clearly reveals his growing debt to de Chirico[2] in the framed painting within the painting and the unreal use of colour to suggest a dreamlike atmosphere. It is particularly noticeable for its photographic realism which gives such credibility to the most irrational subject matter. In his insistence on obeying the dictates of the unconscious, Dali set up his easel at the foot of the bed so that before going to sleep he could fix his mind on the unfinished painting to link his sleep with its further development. At other times he would 'wait whole hours

[1] This was written in the late 1940s, long after the break with Surrealism.

[2] In 1917 de Chirico produced a group of metaphysical interiors in which, against an architectural background, he painted framed pictures within an interior.

Plate 19
Giorgio de Chirico
The Philosophy of Conquest
1914
Art Institute of Chicago

Dali has often made use of de Chirico's deep perspective and the mystery of his shadows, as in *Nostalgic Echo, Illumined Pleasures* (plate 9) and *Outskirts of Paranoiac-Critical Town* (plate 34).

without any such images occurring. Then, not painting, I would remain in suspense ...' or would try by all means possible to simulate madness. Visions of 'three tiny curates running very fast in single file across a little Japanese gangplank ...'[1] would set him off into fits of laughter. Again, he imagined owls perched on peoples' heads, surmounted by pieces of excrement. Free from all reason, he recorded it all with maniacal care.

In the meantime, Camille Goemans arranged to put on his first Paris exhibition late in 1929. The terms were for Dali to receive 3,000 francs for all the works he produced during the summer. Goemans would take a percentage on the sales and have three canvases of his choice. It was an instant success with almost all the paintings sold at between six and twelve thousand francs. *The Lugubrious Game* was bought by the Vicomte de Noailles, who later was to acquire so many of his works.

It was not long before the Surrealists recognised the significant contribution that Dali could now make to the movement. His belief in the superiority of association, the omnipotence of dreams and the

[1]This image was later to be realised in the Dali-Buñuel film *L'Age d'Or*.

Plate 20 **The Phantom Cart**

element of chance were seen as means to an end and an instrument of exploration and discovery. His statement that he was completely uninterested in all aesthetic values and painterly qualities, concerned only with depicting the images of the irrational, was in line with Surrealism's avowed claim that the use of a technique was but a means to an end, that of reconciling man and the universe. During the following weeks Buñuel, Magritte and his wife, Paul Eluard and his wife Gala arrived in Cadaqués. They were distressed by his continuing fits of convulsive laughter and general mental state, and also concerned about his painting *The Lugubrious Game* (plate 6). Eluard suggested Gala approach him on the subject. Did the picture, with its realistic spattering of excrement on the man's back, and to which he showed a particular attachment, refer in any way to his life? Was he in fact a coprophagic? In any case it was felt that the work was weakened by its propaganda as a psychopathological document.

Dali assured her that he had no liking for that type of aberration, but did 'consider scatology as a terrorising element, just as I do blood, or my phobia for grasshoppers'.

This period saw the beginning of his great love for Gala. In his usual way he went to inordinate lengths to attract her. Taking his best shirt he cut it short enough to expose his navel, then tore it on the shoulder and the chest. The collar was entirely removed, his pants turned inside out. Shaving his armpits, they were then dyed with laundry blue. Not completely satisfied, he removed the blue and shaved until his armpits were bloody, then did the same to the knees. For perfume he could find only Eau de Cologne, which made him sick; so he boiled fish glue and water, adding some goat manure and a touch of aspic, making a paste which he rubbed all over his body. He was ready to meet her. Then he saw her through the window and realised that the whole get-up was a nuptial costume. Hurriedly changing, washing off the stench of the concoction as well as possible, he ran to meet her only to collapse at her feet in hysterical laughter.

Gala's initial reaction was not favourable. She thought him obnoxious and unbearable, yet a medium-like intuition told her that his hysteria was not gaiety nor scepticism, but fanaticism. They began to rely increasingly on each other. One day, when he threw himself at her feet, she cried out: 'My little boy! We shall never leave each other.'

Gala. She was born Elena Deluvina Diakanoff, in Russia. She was one of the most fascinating women around the Surrealists during those days. Most of them had been in love with her before her marriage to the poet, Paul Eluard, yet little is really known about her. Like an apparition she appears and disappears, leaving only a fleeting imprint that stirs our imagination. No one has written more about her than Dali. Many of his works are dedicated to her and are frequently signed with their entwined names. Yet she remains remote, always just out of our grasp. When the others returned to Paris, including Eluard, she remained with Dali in Cadaqués.

Plate 20
The Phantom Cart
1933
Oil on panel
6 × 8½ in (15.2 × 21.5 cm)
Edward James Foundation

One of Dali's more lyrical works which preceded the 'Beach at Rosas' series of 1934–1936. The two figures seated in the cart are also the buildings of the distant town, suggesting that the cart has already reached its destination.

Plate 21 **The Ghost of Vermeer of Delft which can be used as a Table**

Dali was now working on a portrait of Paul Eluard and two other large canvases. One was to create a scandal. It represented, he tells us, 'a large head, livid as wax, the cheeks very pink, the eyelashes long, and the impressive nose pressed against the earth This face has no mouth, and in its place was stuck an enormous grasshopper. The grasshopper's belly was decomposed, and full of ants. Several of these ants scurried across the space that should have been filled by the mouth of the great anguished face, whose head terminated in architecture and ornamentations of the style of 1900.' He called the painting *The Great Masturbator*.

His works all packed for his forthcoming exhibition, he again set off for Paris. This time he was to join the Surrealist group.

It is perhaps necessary to pause for a moment while we consider the development of Surrealist painting and the position it had arrived at around the time of Dali's intervention. While it would be impossible to summarise here all the various manifestations that determined the principles on which it rests and continues to build, we can consider some of its fundamental aims.

The first theoretical foundations of Surrealism were laid in 1924, the year of the first Surrealist manifesto, under the direction of André Breton. Surrealism dedicated itself to a far more systematic revision of values and an attitude towards the subconscious as the essential source of all art, following the disruptive and anarchistic action of Dada, which had died in 1922. As a result, a definition was made, dictionary style: 'SURREALISM, n, Pure psychic automatism, by which it is intended to express, verbally, in writing, or by other means, the real process of thought. Thought's dictation, in the absence of all control exercised by reason and outside all aesthetic or moral preoccupations. ENCYCL. philos. Surrealism rests in the belief in the superior reality of certain forms of association neglected heretofore, in the omnipotence of the dream and in the disinterested play of thought. It tends definitely to do away with all other psychic mechanisms and to substitute itself for them in the solution of the principal problems of life.'

The essential spirit of Surrealism, at that time, was clearly formulated. It was a purely intuitive period. 'I believe,' said Breton, 'in the future resolution of the states of dream and reality, in appearance so contradictory, in a sort of absolute reality, or *surréalité*, if I may so call it.'

No conception of Surrealist painting existed then. In fact it was difficult to see how it could transcend 'all aesthetic . . . preoccupations'. Only in automatic writing, in fantasies and states of hallucination could the stream of consciousness emerge. Indeed, Pierre Naville, in 1925, expressed the view that there could be no such thing as Surrealist painting. The whole idea was a contradiction in terms. Breton did not see the definition as quite so rigid. In the same year he published a book, under the still hesitant title *Surrealism and Painting*, in which he declared that 'Painting could supply the rhythmic unity', and there could be an art as 'an instrument of discovery'.

Plate 21
The Ghost of Vermeer of Delft which can be used as a Table
1934
Oil on panel
$7\frac{1}{8} \times 5\frac{1}{2}$ in (18 × 14 cm)
Collection of Mr and Mrs
A. Reynolds Morse, Salvador Dali Museum, Cleveland (Ohio)

Dali's obsession with food and furniture probably prompted this painting, as well as his respect for the art of Vermeer. He has said of this work, 'A spectre that could be used as a table: an eminently eucharistic idea for a painting'.

Surrealist identity would hinge on the methodological and icono-graphic relevance of the picture to the main ideas of the movement – that is, to automatism and the 'dream image'. The automatism of painters like Miró and Masson was the equivalent of the verbal free association which the writer practised. The artist had merely to let his brush wander freely over the surface. 'Rather than setting out to paint something,' Miró explained, 'I begin painting, and as I paint the picture begins to assert itself, or suggest itself under my brush. The form becomes the sign for a woman or a bird as I work . . . The first stage is free, unconcious . . .'

As we see, Surrealism from the beginning excluded the rational and the logical in favour of the irrational. Painters were urged not to draw their inspiration from reality, but from a 'purely interior model' which was defined in those painters who genuinely rediscovered the reason for painting. 'These,' said Breton, 'were Picasso, Max Ernst, Masson, Miró, Tanguy, Arp, Picabia and Man Ray. It was not the artistic quality that was important, but its Surrealist quality. Only its hidden content was of value. This motivation reveals the difference between Surrealist painting and other forms of artistic creation under the sway of aesthetic considerations.'

While automatism still remains today the best-known method of tapping the imaginative resources, the Surrealists were not unaware of the inherent weaknesses in the process. Breton, speaking of the definition of Surrealism made in 1924, admitted '. . . that I deceived myself at the time in advocating the use of an automatic thought not only removed from all control exercised by the reason, but also disengaged from "all aesthetic or moral preoccupations". It should at least have said: "conscious aesthetic or moral preoccupations".' Fascinating though the automatic approach might be, the image has a habit of repeating itself indefinitely. An element of monotony and repetition creeps into unconscious experience. By 1928 many of the Surrealist painters were in the process of working out a method by which the discoveries made by chance could be completed by the intervention of the artist himself, in order to achieve the full realisation of what was inspired by the automatic process. In other words, some degree of control would be necessary.

Dali shared the Surrealists' faith in adapting the automatic pro-cesses to painting, in recording the involuntary images inspired by dreams. He also saw that, for the imagery to achieve its full potential-ity, it had to be developed in a fully conscious way. It did not mean that he arrested the process of free association by which one image suggested another, but that he sought to elaborate his psychic revelations with all the precision and artistic skill at his command, in a conscious and deliberate manner. 'Handmade photography' was the term he used to describe his technique, by which he meant that his painting would be indistinguishable from photography and therefore more believable. Even the size of many of these paintings was no larger than the average photograph.

The Freudian basis of Surrealism was clearly defined between the

Plate 22 **Atmospheric Skull Sodomising a Grand Piano**

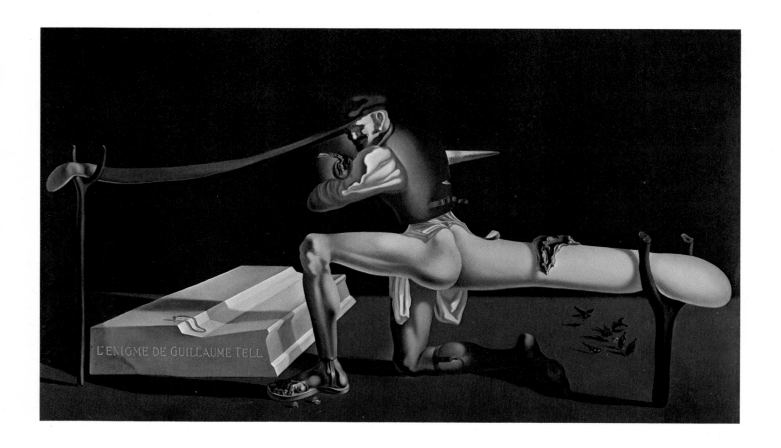

Plate 23
The Enigma of William Tell
1934
Oil on canvas
$78\frac{3}{4} \times 128$ in (200 × 325 cm)
National Museum, Stockholm

The legend of William Tell was re-
interpreted by Dali as one of
incestuous mutilation. Although
devoted to his father, Dali revolted
against his authority, a situation
which eventually led to his being
thrown out of his father's home.
The fond relationship between
father and son in the legend was to
become a thematic obsession for a
number of important works: *William Tell*, painted in 1930, and *The
Old Age of William Tell* of 1931.
This particular painting, in which
Lenin appears trouserless and with
an extended buttock, combined
with Dali's reactionary political
tendencies, was to bring about his
first break with the Surrealists.

Some years later Dali made the
following comment about the painting: 'William Tell, a fatherly phan-
tasm, has placed a mutton chop on
my head, indicating the desire to
eat the infant Dali, whom he carries
in his arms.'

first manifesto of 1924 and the second manifesto of 1929. Technically,
the paintings of that period fall roughly into two groups. The first
is the intuitive, spontaneous approach of Masson and Miró, with its
allegiance to dreams, folly and the incoherent. Breton proposed the
unbridled imagination, and if it contradicted that which was known,
all the better. The second type of Surrealist painting draws on a
meticulously realistic technique by which the identity of the object is
firmly designated. In this category is found the art of such painters
as Magritte, Brauner and Dali. Yet there is one important difference
in Dali's use of his technical ability, namely that he put it at the
service of automatism and passivity. At the same time he was to
revive, with his convincingly illusionist realism, the theory of
painting as an illustrative medium and to champion a return of the
anecdote to art. It was a contribution of major importance to Surrealism
at that time and gave a new impetus to experiments that were still at a
tentative stage.

Breton may have been aware, even that early, of the risks that Dali
might face. In his introduction to the 1929 exhibition he wrote:
'Dali is like a man who hesitates between talent and genius, or as one
might once have said, between vice and virtue. He is one of those who
arrive from so far away that one barely has time to see them enter—
only enter. He takes his place, without saying a word, in a system of
interference.' He continues in a later paragraph: 'On the other hand
there is hope: hope that not everything will become dark even so,
that the admirable voice which is Dali's will not break when it reaches
one's ears, even though certain "materialists" are anxious that the

sound of it should be confused with the creaking of his patent leather shoes ...'[1] Whatever doubts were felt, the importance accorded to him was clearly stated: 'With the coming of Dali, it is perhaps the first time that the mental windows have been opened really wide, so that one can feel oneself gliding up towards the wild sky's trap.'[2]

The originality of Dali, the revolutionary critical interpretation he brought to bear upon familiar works of art, his translating hallucinations and dreams into a concrete reality, and his fascination with all forms of aberration were all essential to Surrealist aims at that time. His understanding of Freud, on which so much of his work was to be based, led to the development of his theories of the 'paranoiac method'. In his book *The Visible Woman* he described it as 'a spontaneous method of irrational knowledge based upon the critical and systematic objectification of delirious associations and interpretations'. In simple terms it was a form of image interpretation, in which the spectator sees in a picture a different image depending on the imaginative ability of the onlooker. For instance, one might see, in a stain on the wall, a face, a castle or a galloping horse. A postcard of a group of negroes sitting around their hut had only to be seen from another angle to become a portrait of André Breton. (Breton insisted it was of the Marquis de Sade.) It was to become the subject for a future painting.

Not unrelated to the paranoiac method is Lautréamont's image, 'beautiful as the chance meeting upon a dissecting table of a sewing machine and an umbrella'. In Freudian terms we recognise the sewing machine as a woman, the umbrella as a man and the dissecting table as a bed. The sewing machine and the umbrella will make love.

Dali envisaged the possibilities of giving objective value on the plane of reality to his world of irrational experiences. The paranoiac-critical activity became a system of revealing images and associations. Like other methods used by the Surrealists, it was a means of forcing inspiration.[3] The interpretative system of paranoiac-critical activity led Dali to transform Millet's *Angelus* into a painting of extreme eroticism. He found that the man on the left was using his hat to hide his turgescent sex, that the woman was pregnant, and that the pitchfork, thrust into the ground alongside the open sack of potatoes, symbolised the male sex and the sack of potatoes the female. Dali maintained that the immense success of the picture, its devout subject matter apart, was entirely due to its latent content.

He was to produce a number of pictures on this theme; for instance, *Gala and the 'Angelus' of Millet Immediately Preceding the Arrival of the Conic Anamorphoses*, illustrated in *Le Surréalisme au Service de la Revolution*, No. 6, 1933, and *Meditation upon the Harp*. Both executed between 1932 and 1935, they are two examples in which he applies the method to the obsessional character of the *Angelus*.

Another artistic theme was launched when he discovered in the legend of William Tell, not the filial devotion that people saw, but incestuous mutilation. It is explored in *William Tell, The Enigma of William Tell* (plate 23) and *The Old Age of William Tell*.

[1] Introduction to the catalogue of the first Dali exhibition, Galerie Goemans, 1929.

[2] Ibid.

[3] The Surrealists made use of a number of automatic processes for this purpose. Decalcomania, or transfer, developed by Dominguez, is a technique in which paint is spread on a sheet of glazed paper, then covered with a similar sheet. After exerting pressure it is slowly lifted, revealing the effect of strange rock formations, mysterious grottoes and coral effects. It was later used by Max Ernst in such paintings as *Napoleon in the Desert*, *The Eye of Silence* and *Europe after the Rain*, around 1937. Fumage was invented by Paalen: a canvas, or any surface, is moved at random above a lighted candle, the smoke being allowed to make marks on the surface. Frottage, used by Max Ernst in 1925, is a matter of applying a sheet of paper or canvas over an uneven surface or object and rubbing with a pencil or crayon, as children do with coins. Ernst's first results were published under the title of *Natural History*. It is important to remember that all these processes were subjected to conscious control by the artist, once the discoveries made by chance were revealed.

Plate 24 **The Weaning of Furniture-Nutrition**

40

Plate 24
The Weaning of Furniture-Nutrition
1934
Oil on panel
7 × 9½ in (17.8 × 24.2 cm)
Collection of Mr and Mrs
A. Reynolds Morse, Salvador Dali
Museum, Cleveland (Ohio)

The back view of the woman is a composite of Dali's childhood nurse and a half-mad fisherwoman named Lidia who lived at Port Lligat and from whom Dali bought a dilapidated fishing hut from which was created his present home. The space cut from the body of the nurse conforms to that of the larger chest which, taken from the woman, might therefore be considered edible. Note the baby's feeding bottle on the small chest.

Plate 25 *overleaf*
L'Omelette Baveuse
1934
Oil on canvas
Private collection

The architecture and ornamentation of Art Nouveau had a profound effect on Dali between the years 1930 and 1934, as can be seen in the ectoplasmic forms in this painting. The irridescent tonality of certain works of the Surrealist painter Yves Tanguy also impressed him at this time.

Plate 26 *overleaf*
Skull with its Lyrical Appendage Leaning on a Night Table which should have the Temperature of a Cardinal's Nest
1934
Oil on panel
9½ × 7½ in (24 × 19 cm)
Private collection

Here a given reality is made to suggest another. The piano keys metamorphose into the teeth of a skull. Such image interpretation was, claimed Dali, entirely due to his 'paranoiac-critical method'.

Plate 25 **L'Omelette Baveuse**

Plate 26 **Skull with its Lyrical Appendage Leaning on a Night Table which should have the Temperature of a Cardinal's Nest**

Plate 27
Mae West
1934–36
Gouache
$10\frac{7}{8} \times 6\frac{7}{8}$ in (27.5 × 17.5 cm)
The Art Institute of Chicago
(Gift of Gilbert W. Chapman)

The furnishings of a room are transformed into a portrait of Mae West. The soft lips were to become a sofa object for Edward James.

Dali's ineffable talent for parading his irrational delirium, his lurid taste for the sensational, was working overtime. He asserted his taste for chromolithographs (a picture printed in colours from stone) as 'the least accidental imitations of nature', and threw light on his own work which was of an 'instantaneous photography in colours and with images that are super-fine, extravagant, extra-plastic, extra-pictorial, unexplored, super-pictorial, super-plastic, deceptive, hyper-normal, feeble and of concrete irrationality'.

It is of course possible to accept the iconography of his work, as Dali himself would insist, without asking what each detail might mean. Yet we know from his own account, not only of his childhood, but of the interpretative studies he has made of Millet, William Tell, the Pre-Raphaelites and others, that there is evidence of a specific meaning behind most of the imagery that finds it way into the paintings. Some, to which he attaches particular importance, are also unforgettable, like the crutches and limp watches. Others, more alarming, he tried to canalise by putting them down on canvas. Grasshoppers, for which he had a morbid fear, identified with dislike for his father. Excrement was seen as 'the terrorising element'. Teeth are a Freudian sex symbol. Blood, forced into his eyes by hanging or swinging his head, provoked retinal illusions. Putrefaction had the hard light of gems. Death he saw as always being beautiful, just as eroticism must always be ugly. Implements, such as sharp instruments, are symbolic of mutilation. He considered that the three cardinal images of life were excrement, blood and putrefaction. 'We have long since learned to recognise the image of desire in images of terror,' said David Gascoyne.[1]

Since his early childhood, Dali was drawn to Vermeer of Delft. No painter has had such a devoted disciple, and Vermeer is probably the only painter he has ever made a copy of. According to Fleur Cowles,[2] the banker-collector Robert Lehman asked him to copy a Vermeer. Dali assured him it was impossible, but in the early 1960s, some twenty years later, in a special room set aside in the Louvre, after exhaustive tests and analysis of colours and pigments, minute study of the way paint was applied down to the width of the brush required, Dali went through a number of violent intellectual efforts to put himself in a state of receptivity. Suddenly he claimed to discover something extraordinary in the painting, which should not have been there. Immediately the experts gathered around with their magnifying glasses, until one discovered the hair from a paint brush hidden between the brush strokes, and the source of Dali's discomfort was revealed. Relieved, he then sat before his canvas and proceeded to draw a rhinoceros horn, in the structure of which he saw the origin of all life. The image recurred in a number of works, including *The Maximum Speed of Raphael's Madonna*; its perfect logarithmic spiral has Platonic implications for Dali.

The influence of Vermeer on his own work is to be seen in a number of paintings: *The Image Disappears*, and more directly in *The Ghost of Vermeer of Delft which can be used as a Table* (plate 21).

[1] *A Short Survey of Surrealism*, Cobden-Sanderson, 1936.

[2] *The Case of Salvador Dali*, 1959.

Plate 27 **Mae West**

Food has always been one of Dali's obsessions.[1] It occurs repeatedly in his autobiography: the prologue opens with, 'At the age of six I wanted to be a cook.' Such words as 'spinach', 'shellfish', 'sturgeon', 'cannibalism', 'bones' and 'caviar' are frequently used to describe painting. It led him to paint a portrait of Gala with two lamb chops on her shoulder, as well as *The Weaning of Furniture-Nutrition* (plate 24). Cooking turkey without killing it was one of his culinary refinements, and once he conceived the idea of making a table of egg-white so that it could be eaten. 'Cooking is very close to painting,' he insists. His devotion to food and Vermeer might explain why *The Ghost of Vermeer* (plate 21) suggests that it could be used as a dining table. If Vermeer has top marks in his gallery of painters, Velásquez runs him a close second, failing only in inspiration and mystery.[2] Applying his paranoiac-critical facility, he saw the apparition of Velásquez's Infanta in the top of a Hindu temple. More significantly, it is Velásquez's technical brilliance and richness of colour that are the lyrical inspiration for *Apparition of Face and Fruit-dish on a*

[1]*Les Diners de Gala,* with 136 recipes by Dali, has been published by Felicie Inc.

[2]*Fifty Secrets of Magic Craftsmanship,* Salvador Dali, 1948.

Plate 28 **Paranoiac-Critical Solitude**

Beach (plate 43). The painting is also an exploration into the use of the multiple image. The base of the fruit-dish is a back view of his childhood nurse to form the nose and mouth of the face, while the fruit and the coastline are metamorphosed into a dog.

History provides many such examples of the fantastic in art: distorted perspective, composite images, Bosch's highly personal visions, and the use of the double image by the late 16th-century painter Arcimboldo (plate 41). They were all put to a use by the Surrealists who had first rejected the rational basis on which these techniques were founded. Tearing away the curtain, they demonstrated that every form of the strange and mad could work in the cause of art and transport it outside its own limits. Dali's acceptance of every form of madness took him further than the other Surrealists. By simulating the disordered mind of the paranoiac, he became hypersensitive to hidden appearances and counter-appearances, seeing not two or three images but a sequence of images limited only by the mind's capacity. In *The Endless Enigma* six concealed images are represented in the painting. Less complex is *Old Age, Adolescence, Infancy*. Dali maintained that the delirious image suggested by an initial object might be the true reality. In *La Femme Visible* he wrote: 'I challenge materialists to enquire into the more complex problem as to which of these images has the highest probability of existence if the intervention of desire is taken into account.' The 'omnipotence of desire,' said Breton, 'has remained, since the beginning, Surrealism's sole act of faith.' The intensity of Dali's hallucinatory powers makes others believe in the reality of what he sees. In truth he could say that the putrefaction of a donkey can be considered as 'the hard and blinding flash of new gems'.

One of his more subtle uses of the double image is to be seen in the painting entitled *Spain* (plate 42). The group of horsemen and figures

Plate 28
Paranoiac-Critical Solitude
1935
Oil on panel
$7\frac{1}{2} \times 9\frac{1}{8}$ in (19 × 23 cm)
Edward James Foundation

Dali's dislike of all mechanical things led him to declare in his manifesto, *Declaration of the Independence of the Imagination and of the Rights of Man to his own Madness*: 'Only the violence and duration of your hardened dream can resist the hideous mechanical civilisation that is your enemy . . .'; and again: 'The history of the true creative artist is filled with the abuses and encroachments by means of which an absolute tyranny is imposed by the industrial mind over the new creative ideas of the poetic mind.'

The treatment of the car in this painting is characteristic of his contempt for the mechanical and for industrialism. Here the vehicle has been excavated fossil-like from the rock.

Plate 29
Joan Miró
The Carnival of Harlequin
1924–25
Albright-Knox Art Gallery, Buffalo (N.Y.)

Miró was one of the first Surrealist painters. His work represents the intuitive, spontaneous approach as opposed to the realistic, which Dali was to introduce into Surrealism in 1929.

47

in combat, forming the face of the woman, owes an unmistakeable debt to Leonardo, another painter of the past whom he now admired. They both shared a common foundation of inventiveness. And Dali was undoubtedly familiar with Freud's study of Leonardo, as well as that artist's advice to look at the damp stains on walls in which one might see all kinds of strange and imaginary images.

'The abject misery of abstract creation'[1] is the chapter heading to Dali's attack on abstract art. He saw in it a lack of philosophic and general culture and evidence of mental debility, offering us 'upon the fresh optimism of their shiny paper the soup of the abstract aesthetic, which really and truly is even worse than the cold and colossally sordid vermicelli soups of neo-theism, which even the most convulsively hungry cats would not go near'.

As an antidote to its influence and to that of Negro art, which Picasso and other painters were extolling in Paris, Dali upheld the decoration and architecture of 'Art Nouveau', which he considered as 'the psychopathological end-product of the Greco-Roman decadence', finding in the ornamentation of the entrances to the Paris

[1] *The Conquest of the Irrational.*

Plate 30 **Medianimic-Paranoiac Image**

48

Plate 30
Medianimic-Paranoiac Image
1935
Oil on panel
$7\frac{1}{2} \times 9\frac{1}{8}$ in (19 × 23 cm)
Edward James Foundation

Another painting of the Rosas series in which the fixtures take on a phantom-like effect.

Plate 31
Morphological Echo
1936
Oil on panel
12 × 13 in (30.5 × 33 cm)
Collection of Mr and Mrs A. Reynolds Morse, Salvador Dali Museum, Cleveland (Ohio)

Plate 32
Lobster-Telephone
1936
12 × 6 × 3 in (30 × 15 × 7 cm)
Edward James Foundation

Dali made a number of Surrealist objects for his English patron, Edward James, including the famous 'Lobster-Telephone'. It illustrates his fascination with giving life to the inanimate.

Plate 33
Three Young Surrealist Women Holding in their Arms the Skins of an Orchestra
1936
Oil on canvas
21¼ × 25⅝ in (54 × 65 cm)
Collection of Mr and Mrs A. Reynolds Morse, Salvador Dali Museum, Cleveland (Ohio)

Plate 34
Outskirts of Paranoiac-Critical Town
1936
Oil on panel
18⅛ × 26 in (46 × 66 cm)
Edward James Foundation

The outline of the distant bell tower is duplicated in the foreground structure, through which is seen the skipping girl who also becomes the bell in the tower. Dali made a painting of this detail in 1935, called *Nostalgic Echo*. There is also a portrait of Gala holding up a bunch of grapes.

[1] Equally compulsive are the architectural structures of the Postman Cheval, who built his dream palace at Hauterives in France. Between 1879 and 1912 he collected stones in his postman's bag and laboriously over the years constructed his dream.

Metro a wrought iron vegetation full of mystery, eroticism and perversity. The imaginative dream structures of Antonio Gaudí in Barcelona, houses 'created for madmen, for erotomaniacs', were very familiar to Dali. The Parc Güell, and the Basilica of the Church of the Holy Family suggested 'in the most material way the persistence of dreams in the face of reality'.[1]

Many of the 'undulant-convulsive' forms in his paintings between 1930 and 1934 are traceable to the ornamental elements of the 1900 'Modern Style'. In the faces of these hysterical sculptures he saw those madwomen, treated by Dr Charcot, at the mental hospital of Saltpetrière.

The treatment of what gives all the appearance of petrified hair on two images in *The Font* has the delirium associated with the more extreme excesses of that style, and he also made significant use of its compositional motifs. The painting shows, too, his growing interest in the emotive value of deep perspective that he saw in certain canvases of de Chirico. But whereas de Chirico was motivated by the mystery hiding behind normal relationships, Dali evokes a delirious world of clinical irrationality bathed in an irridescent light. What he does share with de Chirico is the ability to project his apparent dislocations with the same acceptability, in spite of the inordinate nature of the imagery. *The Invisible Man*, which he started in 1929, did not escape the influence of Art Nouveau, recognisable in the treatment of the 'vaginal head' of the figure, as well as the sensuous ornamentation of the foreground.

There is little doubt that Dali's theories and plastic involvement with this style led to a revival of interest and a reappraisal of the movement. Nothing would have pleased him more than the public reaction in 1895 to the first Art Nouveau posters of Alphonse Mucha: 'le délire ... le délire de la laideur' ('delirium ... delirium of the

Plate 33 **Three Young Surrealist Women Holding in their Arms the Skins of an Orchestra**

Plate 34 **Outskirts of Paranoiac-Critical Town**

Plate 35 **Autumn Cannibalism**

ugly'). It was nevertheless a discouraging period for Dali. The sale of his paintings following the Goeman's exhibition was not going well, which he blamed on 'the freemasonry of modern art'. Goemans had gone into bankruptcy owing him money. If the public would not buy his works, perhaps they would buy his inventions. Each day Gala would walk the streets of Paris with a portfolio of drawings for such items as transparent mannequins for shop windows, their bodies filled with water and live goldfish, bakelite furniture shaped to fit the body contours, shoes with springs to augment the pleasure of walking, artificial fingernails made of tiny reducing mirrors in which one saw oneself, dresses with false insets and anatomical padding to titillate man's erotic fantasies. Rejected as uncommercial at the time, many were to make their appearance as a result of his influence, for which he received no credit.

Dali was to carry out many Surrealist objects for the English collector, Edward James, whom he called 'the humming-bird poet'. The Mae West sofa, made in the shape of her lips and taken from the portrait he made of her, the famous lobster telephone and, in James's country house in Sussex, the white grand piano rising from the centre of a pond with jets of water spouting from the keyboard.

As early as 1914 Marcel Duchamp[1] has chosen 'ready-mades' and 'aided ready-mades' which could be considered the first Surrealist objects. In 1924 André Breton had suggested the making of certain objects which one only sees in dreams. In the following years Surrealism was to draw attention to various categories of objects: the found object, interpreted object, phantom object, poem object and the object functioning symbolically, invented by Dali, which were based on phantasmagoria and representations produced by unconscious acts. These objects were intended to procure by indirect means a particular sexual emotion and, by calling on Dali's ultra-confusing activity rising out of the obsessing idea, led to the creation of such objects as *Retrospective Bust of a Woman Devoured by Ants*, *The Aphrodisiac Jacket*, to which fifty wine glasses filled with crème de menthe and a dead fly had been attached, and *Atmospheric Chair*, with a seat composed of bars of chocolate. On a more ambitious level were the two hundred live, edible snails which crawl over a semi-nude figure in an ivy-wreathed taxi.

Dali's shoe fetish goes back to his adolescence and appears in many paintings and objects. Schiaparelli created a hat in the form of a shoe based on an idea by him. It is an object 'most charged with realistic virtues as opposed to musical objects which I have always tried to represent as demolished, crushed, soft-cellos of rotten meat ...'

The Surrealist object, Dali maintained, discredited completely the dream period of Surrealism, and the meaningless writing dictated by the unconscious. He saw the object as a new reality, useless from a practical point of view but 'created wholly for the purpose of materialising in a fetishistic way, with the maximum of tangible reality, ideas and fantasies having a delirious character'. People would no longer

Plate 35
Autumn Cannibalism
1936–37
Oil on canvas
$31\frac{1}{2} \times 31\frac{1}{2}$ in (80 × 80 cm)
Edward James Foundation (on loan to the Tate Gallery, London)

One of Dali's most remarkable works and an astonishing triumph of imagination. Food has always been one of Dali's obsessions: 'Cooking is very close to painting,' he once said. 'When you are making a dish you add a little of this and a little of that ... it's like mixing paints.' In this painting of two beings in the act of devouring each other appear a number of familiar Dalian images – crutches, bread, ants as well as the instruments of mutilation.

[1] Although the marginal role of Marcel Duchamp in Surrealism is outside the scope of this book, his contribution to the movement had a certain validity for a time, in particular the anti-art objects distinguished by their banality. It was, however, his obsessive need to supply written confirmation of his philosophical speculations which was later on to bring him to the attention of the abstract artists of the 'establishment' modern school, many of whom now live off his projects and utterances.

Plate 36
Metamorphosis of Narcissus
1936–37
Oil on canvas
20 × 30 in (50.8 × 76.3 cm)
Edward James Foundation (on
loan to the Tate Gallery, London)

Dali explained this painting to
Freud, when they met in London
in 1938, prompting Freud to re-
mark: 'I have never seen a more
complete example of a Spaniard.
What a fanatic!' The work was
literally illustrated by a poem Dali
wrote at the same time, on the
theme of the death and fossilisation
of Narcissus.

face the limitations of only talking about their manias and phobias,
'but could now touch them, manipulate and operate them with their
own hands'.

He also planned a number of bread objects. 'Not,' he maintained,
'precisely intended for the succour and sustenance of large families.
My bread was a ferociously anti-humanitarian bread, it was the
bread of the revenge of imaginative luxury on the utilitarianism of the
rational practical world...' It was to be aristocratic, paranoiac,
paralysir g and phenomenal. One idea in true Dali style was to bake a
loaf fifteen metres long, which was to be placed, wrapped in newspaper, in the gardens of the Palais Royal. The public reaction and
speculation was then to be reported in detail. Next day a loaf twenty

Plate 37 *overleaf*
Sleep
1937
Oil on canvas
20 × 30¾ in (50.8 × 78.2 cm)
New Trebizond Foundation

Dali saw sleep as a monster supported by crutches.

metres long would be found in the court of Versailles, to be followed
by thirty-metre loaves appearing simultaneously in the public squares
of various capitals of Europe.

For the first New York World's Fair in 1939 Dali's *Dream of Venus*
involved seventeen live mermaids in a water-filled tank: some milked
an underwater cow, others played pianos or were answering telephones. Obeying only the laws of chance or of psychic necessity, such
objects established a canon of the unexpected, lending coherence to
a dream world which identified itself with a new exciting and poetic
experience. They demonstrated the validity of Lautréamont's
contention that poetry can be made by all.

Dali's ceaseless intervention into all aspects of Surrealist activity —

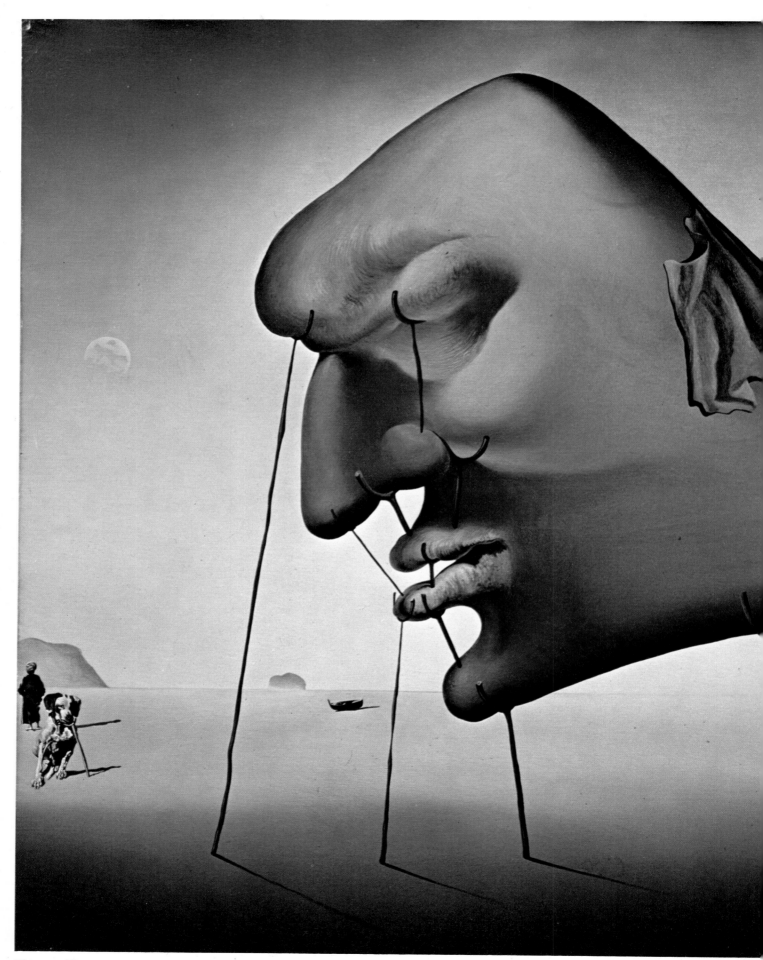

Plate 37 **Sleep**

Plate 38
Hieronymus Bosch
The Garden of Earthly Delights
Right-hand panel
Oil on wood
The Prado, Madrid

There have been many attempts to
see Dali as the Hieronymus Bosch
of our time, an error he has cor-
rected in the following statement:
'Bosch's monsters are the product
of fog-shrouded Nordic forests and
the awful indigestion of the Middle
Ages. The results are symbolic
characters, and satire took advan-
tage of that gigantic diarrhoea. It's
a universe I'm not interested in. In
fact it's the exact opposite of
monsters who are born in a different
way and who, on the contrary, issue
from the overplus of Mediterranean
light.'

Plate 39
Inventions of the Monsters
1937
Oil on canvas
$20\frac{1}{8} \times 30\frac{7}{8}$ in (51×78.5 cm)
The Joseph Winterbotham
Collection, Art Institute of
Chicago

Dali's interest in the Italian masters
and in established aesthetic values
began to have an impact on his
work. To the 'great Realists', like
Velásquez and Vermeer of Delft, he
now added Leonardo, as in the
foreground figure, recognisable as
Leonardo's Madonna. The two
figures seated alongside are portraits of the artist and Gala.

his critical writing, painting, his objects and poetry – were all essential contributions to the vitality of the movement. His obsession with all aspects of visual phenomena and his fascination with giving life to the inanimate and seeking out hidden biological meanings have formed the theses for his ideological inspiration, 'a Renaissance man converted to psychoanalysis', according to Sarane Alexandrian.[1]

Only in a few instances has Dali offered any explanation as to the meaning of his paintings. In *Conquest of the Irrational* he wrote: 'The fact that I myself, at the moment of painting, do not understand my own pictures does not mean that these pictures have no meaning; on the contrary, their meaning is so profound, complex, coherent and involuntary that it escapes the most simple analysis of logical intuition. To describe my pictures in everyday language, to explain them, it is necessary to submit them to special analyses, and preferably with the most ambitiously objective scientific rigour possible. Then all explanation arises *a posteriori* once the picture already exists as a phenomenon.' The disquieting limp watches in *The Persistence of Memory* (plate 14) came into being as a result of eating Camembert cheese, with its particular softness. 'You may be sure that the famous soft watches are nothing else than the tender, extravagant, solitary, paranoiac-critical Camembert of time and space.' Marcel Jean[2] gives a more illuminating explanation. 'The word *montre* (watch) is a word-image with a double meaning: in French, it is the imperative

[1] *Surrealist Art,* Thames & Hudson, London, 1970.

[2] *The History of Surrealist Painting,* Editions de Seuil, Paris, 1959.

Plate 39 **Inventions of the Monsters**

Plate 40 **Palladio's Corridor of Thalia**

of the verb *montrer* (to show) and the name of the apparatus *montrant* (showing) the time. But there is a very common childhood experience: the doctor asks the sick child to *montrer sa langue* (show his tongue), which obviously is soft. The child, we may say, *la montre molle* (shows it soft, with the double sense that in French this phrase can also mean 'the soft watch'). The irrational and even anguished nature of this act for the child, in view of the circumstances, could certainly constitute an experience capable of leaving profound impressions in the psyche. Here, then, is a most concrete origin for the image of the soft watches, an origin founded in an authentic childhood memory, which seems to be confirmed by the titles of the picture ...' Bought by the American gallery owner Julien Levy, it was sold and resold until it was finally hung in the Museum of Modern Art, New York. It was to achieve such popular success that reproductions were used to attract custom to furniture and vegetable shops.

A few years later he was to paint *The Spectre of Sex Appeal* with his explanation 'of having predicted in 1928, at the height of the cult for functional and practical anatomy, in the midst of the most shocking scepticism, the imminence of the round and salivary muscles of Mae West, viscous and terrible with hidden biological meanings. Today I announce that all the new sexual allure of women will come from the possible utilisation of their capacities and resources as ghosts, that is to say, their possible dissociation, their charnel and luminous decomposition.' Now women with sex appeal would have detachable portions of their anatomy, which they could hand round for admiration. It seems unlikely that this painting is the result of hypnotic trance or hallucination so much as an attempt, in clear consciousness, to realise one of his inspired ideas. It is conceived in brilliant colours, because he wanted it to be 'more beautiful and terrifying than the white truffle of death: a rainbow'. The image of the crutches that support the spectre, and appear in many later paintings, began when he was a child staying with Señor Pitchot. Dali sees the crutch fetish in two ways: firstly sociologically, for a wealthy but weak society in need of support; secondly he sees in the shape of the crutch the significance of life and death – a support for his imagined feeling of inadequacy. The monstrous bodiless head of *Sleep* (plate 37) is propped up with innumerable crutches, not only raising it off the ground but holding its features – lips, nose and eyes. He speaks of them as 'wooden supports derived from Cartesian philosophy. Generally used as a support for the tenderness of soft structure.'

By 1934 Dali had directed his attention to what he was to call 'instantaneous' figures, possibly inspired by the particular effect of sunlight that is found on the beach at Rosas, situated a few miles from Figueras, although in his memoirs he talks of painting a few apparently very normal paintings, 'inspired by the congealed and minute enigma of certain snapshots, to which I added a Dalinian touch of Meissonier ...' The ostensible subject matter could certainly have been released

Plate 40
Palladio's Corridor of Thalia
1937
Oil on canvas
46¼ × 35⅝ in (117.5 × 90.5 cm)
Edward James Foundation

Palladio's stage sets for the Teatro Olimpico in Vicenza, with their dramatic use of perspective, have been transformed by Dali into human forms. He was to paint another variation on the theme, *Palladio's Corridor of Dramatic Surprise*, in 1938. Since the animate and the inanimate are indistinguishable according to his 'paranoiac' ability, Dali sees no reason why such inanimate objects as chests, telephones and in this case architecture should not assume living forms.

Plate 41
Giuseppe Arcimboldo
Summer
1563
Kunstistorisches Museum, Vienna

The ambiguous double-image was used by many artists of the 16th and 17th centuries. It was to play an important part in Dali's iconography, and through his 'paranoiac-critical method' he was able to recognise hidden meanings in the most unlikely subjects.

Plate 42
Spain
1938
Oil on canvas
$36 \times 23\frac{5}{8}$ in (91.5 × 60 cm)
New Trebizond Foundation

Dali's use of the multiple image is a genuine *tour de force*. The equestrian battle in the distance, influenced by Leonardo, is so arranged as to form the face of the woman leaning on the chest in the foreground.

by seeing old snapshots of his childhood and memories of being with his nurse on the beach. These figures are, possibly, phantoms, sublimated versions, as Freud has said, of 'the nocturnal visitors attired in nightdresses, who awoke the child to put him on the chamberpot so that he should not wet the bed, or who lifted the bedclothes in order to see how he held his hands in sleep'. An important feature in the works of this period is the stereoscopic effect produced by these figures against a background, as well as the complete lack of distortion in the treatment. Also discernible is a distinct move towards aesthetic values. *Paranoiac-Astral Image*, *Apparition on the Beach at Rosas*, as well as *Noon*, although free of his usual mannerisms and fetishistic devices, achieve an apparitional effect and project a condition of apprehension that is recognised in hallucinations or in dreams. They capture a haunting premonition of a secret activity that lies midway between actual reality and the magic realm of unconscious desires.

Plate 42 **Spain**

Plate 43 **Apparition of a Face and Fruit-dish on a Beach**

Not unrelated to the Rosas series of paintings is one of his most strikingly poetic works, *The Phantom Cart* (plate 20), in which we see that the back of the two figures seated in the cart are really part of the buildings in the distant town. By some strange alchemy, the cart has already reached its destination while it is still some way off.

On the occasion of the Surrealist exhibition at the Galerie Colle in 1933, Dali had proposed a catalogue preface praising the art of Meissonier, a popular academic of the last century, for his 'irrational exactness'. Opposition among the Surrealists was unanimous. They saw little purpose in recognising such a painter as a model of Surrealism. More disquieting was Dali's interest in Nazism and Hitler's rise to power in Germany.[1] A 'Hitlerian nurse' had made its appearance in certain works, while in *The Enigma of William Tell* (plate 23) a portrait of Lenin appeared, without any trousers and with an extended buttock supported by a crutch. It was to show a very different tribute from *Six Apparitions of Lenin on a Piano* (plate 13), painted in the previous year. *Six Apparitions*, for all its complex imagery, could be taken as a sign of Dali's sympathy with Surrealism's political leanings. Understandably, though, such works by the Surrealists were not likely to meet with the Communists' approval, who believed in a Social Realist art, and this soon led to a break between the groups, with the formation of an 'Association of Revolutionary Writers and Artists' by the Surrealists, which Dali refused to join.

In the political climate of the time, with Surrealism taking a more positive attitude against the forces of capitalism, changing *La Revolution Surrealiste* to *Le Surrealisme au Service de la Revolution* ('Surrealism in the Service of the Revolution'), Dali's uneasy relationship with the movement, following the success of his first exhibition in New York at the Julien Levy Gallery, which had identified him as the only authentic voice of Surrealism, along with his growing interest in the aristocracy, monarchy and Catholicism, led to a confrontation with the Surrealists at a meeting in André Breton's house.

Accounts vary on what took place at this meeting. Some say he was officially expelled, others that he was being censured for the wilder eccentricities. Dali turned up with a thermometer in his mouth, pretending to have 'flu. As the discussion became more heated, he kept checking his temperature, and with each attack on him proceeded to take off one of the numerous shirts he was wearing until, naked to the waist, he threw himself at Breton's feet. Dali's defence was that his obsession with Hitler was purely paranoid and apolitical, and he would probably be one of the first to be done away with as a degenerate, if Europe was conquered. Not all the Surrealists were unanimous in their opposition, and Dali succeeded so well in creating an atmosphere of confusion and hysteria that the affair eventually petered out. Although Dali no longer attended the meetings, he was still invited to contribute to the group's exhibitions, including the controversial portrait of Lenin, which was shown at the Galerie Bonjean in 1934.

It was nevertheless the first sign, which Breton had already

Plate 43
Apparition of Face and Fruit-dish on a Beach
1938
Oil on canvas
$45 \times 57\frac{1}{2}$ in (114×146 cm)
E. G. and M. C. Sumner Collection, Wadsworth Atheneum, Hartford (Connecticut)

The multiple image is revealed in a sequence of subjects. The base of the dish is also the back view of his nurse of the Rosas series, which in turn also becomes a face. The dog's head is part of the beach, its back composed of fruit. Dali wrote: 'The double image may be extended, continuing the paranoiac advance, and then the presence of another dominant idea is enough to make a third image appear, and so on, until there is a number of images limited only by the mind's degree of paranoiac capacity.'

[1]Although Dali kept silent during the Spanish civil war, his sympathy was with Franco. Since the last war he has again expressed his admiration for Hitler.

Plate 44 **Impressions of Africa**

detected when he wrote the introduction to Dali's first Paris exhibition. But 'the sound of Dali's admirable voice' was to last only a few more years. In the meanwhile he continued to enrich the movement with his researches.

Between 1933 and 1936, Dali applied his mental and plastic resources to a number of inspirational sources, as well as making literary contributions to *Minotaure*, and to *Cahiers d'Art* for which he wrote an article on Surrealist objects. He began to explore various skeletal and cephalic deformations, in which figures take on grotesquely deformed growths. *Average Atmospherocephalic Bureaucrat in the Act of Milking a Cranial Harp, Myself at the Age of Ten when I was the Grasshopper Child*, as well as *Meditation on the Harp*, are typical examples of his clinical imagination, made all the more disturbing because of our knowledge that certain people are victims of such disfigurations.

It was not difficult to see in the slightly ridiculous figure, without trousers, in the act of milking the soft monstrosity, a clearly masturbatory image, while *Meditation on the Harp* draws on the devout image of the man in Millet's *Angelus* being embraced by a voluptuous nude as he hides an erection behind his hat.

In only one instance, inspired by these deformations, *Soft Construction with Boiled Beans: Premonition of Civil War*, which was painted in 1936, did Dali offer some explanation of his thoughts: 'I showed a vast human body breaking out into monstrous excrescences of arms and legs tearing at one another in a delirium of auto-strangulation. As a background to this architecture of frenzied flesh devoured by a narcissistic and biological cataclysm, I painted a geological landscape, that had been uselessly revolutionised for thousands of years, congealed in its "normal course". The soft structure of that great mass of flesh in civil war I embellished with a few boiled beans, for one could not imagine swallowing all that unconscious meat without the presence (however uninspiring) of some mealy and melancholy vegetable.'

Another approximation of his obsession with elongated growths supported by a crutch is *The Javanese Mannequin*, with its delicately wrought skeletal body.

Among the figures of rhetoric, there is one known as catachresis, by which the imagination supplies a known word to partially describe a new object – for instance, we speak of the foot of a table, or the arm of a windmill, taking from two different objects the means to create a third one. The Oxford *Shorter English Dictionary* gives as an example, 'Lakes by the figure catachresis called seas'. Used in a visual sense, they could be described as lyrical relations, when the outline of a hill and a reclining nude are interchangeable. Less familiar among Dali's works is a small painting entitled *Skull with its Lyrical Appendage Leaning on a Night Table which should have the Temperature of a Cardinal's Nest* (plate 26), showing a liquefying piano, its black and white keyboard stretched in such a manner that the keys metamorphose into the teeth of an adjoining skull. In a more restrained

Plate 44
Impressions of Africa
1938
Oil on canvas
36 × 46¼ in (91.5 × 117.5 cm)
Edward James Foundation (on loan to the Tate Gallery, London)

'Africa accounts for something in my work, since without having been there I remember so much about it!'

Dali had certainly read Raymond Roussel's *Impressions of Africa*, which are entirely imaginary, and which he said had been inspired by some opera glasses with the bazaar of Cairo painted on one lens and the bazaar of Luxor on the other.

The brushwork shows the influence of Velásquez. The figure at the easel is a self-portrait and a number of double images are evident in the background.

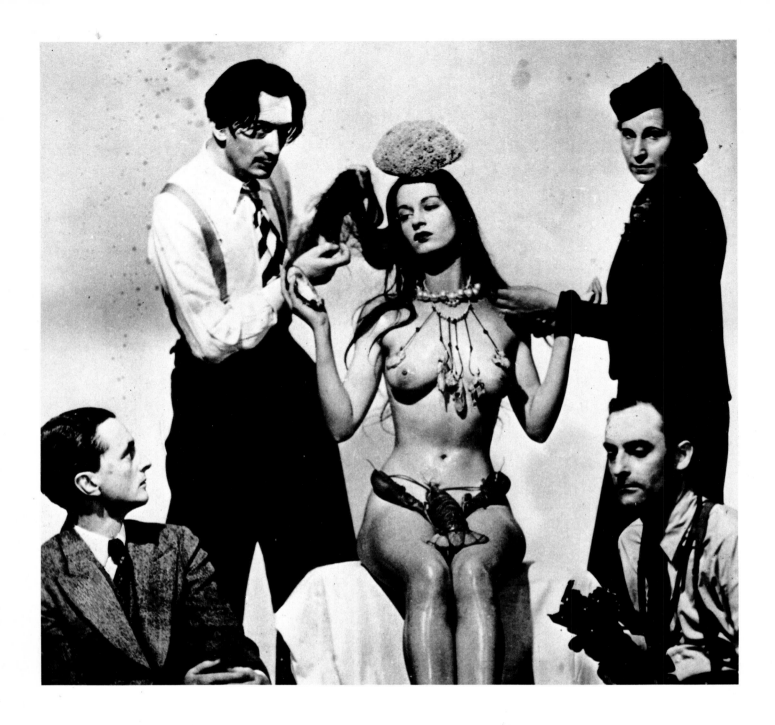

Plate 45
Dali and Gala arranging a living
mannequin for the New York
World Fair in 1939.

vein is *Nostalgic Echo* in which the outline of the young girl skipping
is repeated in the shape of the bell in the tower and in the keyhole
in the chest, while the shape of the wall in the foreground is repeated
in the bell tower itself. Dali's debt to de Chirico is again recognisable
in the girl skipping and the shadow of an unseen presence. It is a
direct allusion to the most marvellous of de Chirico's paintings,
The Mystery and Melancholy of a Street. The reference is further
strengthened by its stillness, the feeling that time itself is frozen,
with everything bathed in a strange melancholy.

It was not until 1931 that the first important exhibition of Surrealism was to take place outside of France. An American show
was quickly followed by Dali's one-man exhibition in Barcelona.
Then E. L. T. Mesens initiated another group show in Brussels in

1934. From then onwards Surrealist exhibitions became frequent–Copenhagen, Prague, Tokyo, Tenerife, Holland–and groups were formed in some fifteen countries. In June 1936 a large international exhibition was opened in the New Burlington Galleries, London. Organised by Roland Penrose, with the collaboration of the French and Belgian groups, it brought together pictures, objects, drawings, collages, sculptures, African and American primitive objects as well as children's drawings. Dali was represented by twelve works, including the *Retrospective Bust of a Woman* and *Aphrodisiac Jacket*.

During the opening, a young woman wandered through the gallery dressed in a white gown, her head and face completely covered with roses on which rested live ladybirds. She wore long black surgical gloves and carried a model human leg in one hand and a raw pork chop in the other.[1] The exhibition was opened by André Breton, dressed in green, smoking a green pipe, accompanied by his wife with long green hair. During the exhibition Dali was to give a lecture in a diving suit, which had been rented by Lord Berners for the occasion. When he was asked to specify the depth of the descent, he replied that Mr Dali was going to descend to the unconscious. In that case, the suppliers assured him, they would replace the usual helmet with a special one. Dali appeared in the suit, decorated with plasticine hands, a radiator cap on top of the helmet, a dagger in the belt and holding

Plate 46
Slave Market with Disappearing Bust of Voltaire
1940
Oil on canvas
$18\frac{1}{4} \times 25\frac{3}{4}$ in (46.3 × 65.5 cm)
Collection of Mr and Mrs
A. Reynolds Morse, Salvador Dali
Museum, Cleveland (Ohio)

Voltaire's face appears in a number of works. Here it will be recognised in the two figures dressed in black, whose faces go to form the eyes of Voltaire. The area of sky seen through the irregular arch behind them forms the head.

[1]In Marcel Jean's *History of Surrealist Painting*, she is shown in Trafalgar Square among the pigeons.

Plate 46 **Slave Market with Disappearing Bust of Voltaire**

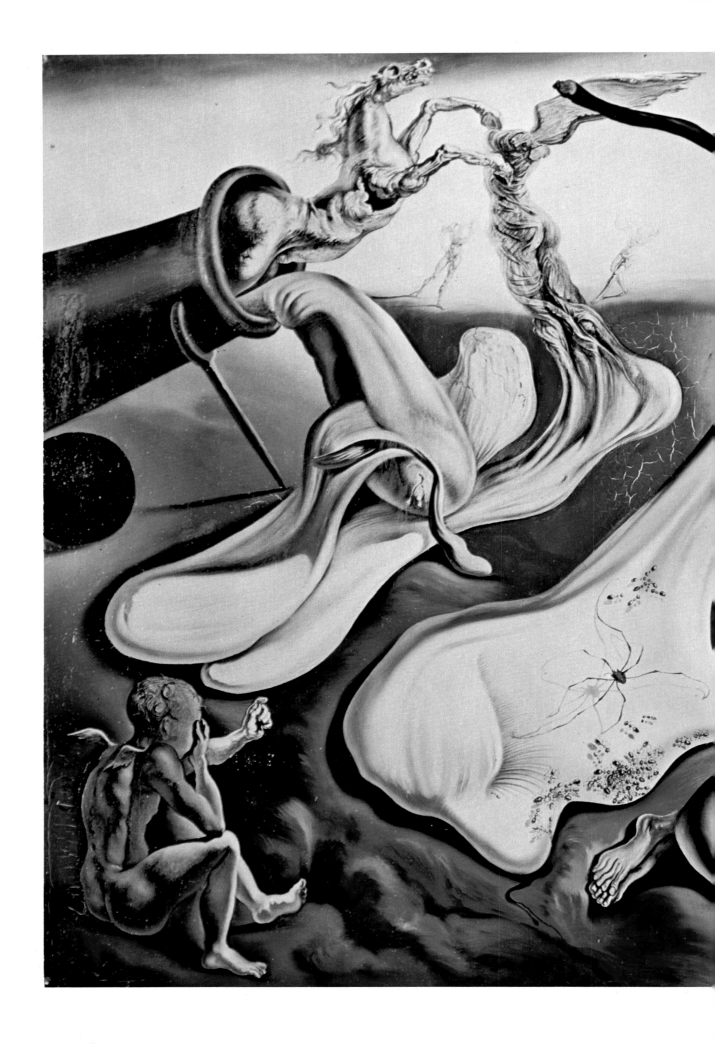

Plate 47
Daddy Long Legs–Hope
1940
Oil on canvas
16 × 20 in (40.5 × 50.8 cm)
Private collection

two Russian wolfhounds on leads. After trying to deliver his lecture, quite inaudibly from inside the helmet, Dali, dripping with perspiration and nearly suffocating from lack of air, gestured wildly to have the helmet removed, only to discover that the mechanic had locked the bolts so securely that no one could remove it.

The end of this year saw a number of works, among which was the remarkable painting *Autumn Cannibalism* (plate 35), in which a liquefying figure spreads itself over a chest, as it eats itself with a knife and fork. One of Dali's great contributions was to show the chaotic background to the work of art; mitigated by aesthetic control his pictures would not be what they are, and while much of his work might be considered external documentation, *Autumn Cannibalism* is a triumph of imagination. It is as though he has translated all the desires of humanity into flesh and not as usual into form.

It was two years later, in London, that Dali realised one of his greatest ambitions, to meet Sigmund Freud, made possible with the help of Stefan Zweig. While crossing the yard on the day of the meeting, Dali reported, 'I saw a bicycle leaning against the wall, and on the saddle, attached by a string, was a red rubber hot-water bottle, which looked full of water and on the back of the hot-water bottle walked a snail.'[1]

Freud, then seriously ill, is reported to have made only two remarks: 'In classic paintings, I look for the sub-conscious—in a Surrealist painting, for the conscious.' As his guests left, he turned to Zweig, saying: 'I have never seen a more complete example of a Spaniard. What a fanatic.' Dali was later to claim that Freud's pronouncement on Surrealist painting was a death sentence for the doctrine. From now on it was to be not experimentation but tradition, not revolution but renaissance.

Dali's patron, Edward James, bought many of his works during that period, and he was a frequent guest at James's house. At that time his English was practically non-existent, which could account for the misunderstanding that arose upon hearing someone talk of 'a chest of drawers'. Interpreting this quite literally, Dali in *Anthropomorphic Cabinet* as well as a number of drawings, was to show a reclining woman out of whose chest appeared numerous half-open drawers. The idea could have been supplemented by an awareness of the 17th-century drawings of Bracelli, showing the human figure constructed of such items as boxes, tennis rackets and bell towers.

Few artists have shown their contempt for the machine so strongly as Dali. Contemporary industrial products are invariably treated with savage disregard for their natural properties, either by transforming them into living forms, or by reducing them to the fury of disintegration. The motor car which appears in a number of his works never looks as though it will run, and in *Paranoiac-Critical Solitude* (plate 28) it has been excavated, fossil-like, from the rock. 'Machines are doomed to crumble and rust,' he claimed. Mechanical brains like

Plate 48
Geopoliticus Child Watching the Birth of the New Man
1943
Oil on canvas
18 × 20½ in (45.7 × 52 cm)
Collection of Mr and Mrs
A. Reynolds Morse, Salvador
Dali Museum, Cleveland (Ohio)

Dali's decision to become classical and to 'paint pictures uniquely consecrated to the architecture of the Renaissance and the Special Sciences' was made in 1941, and a growing academicism in his technique became noticeable.

[1] He had earlier discovered that Freud's cranium was a snail—a spiral brain.

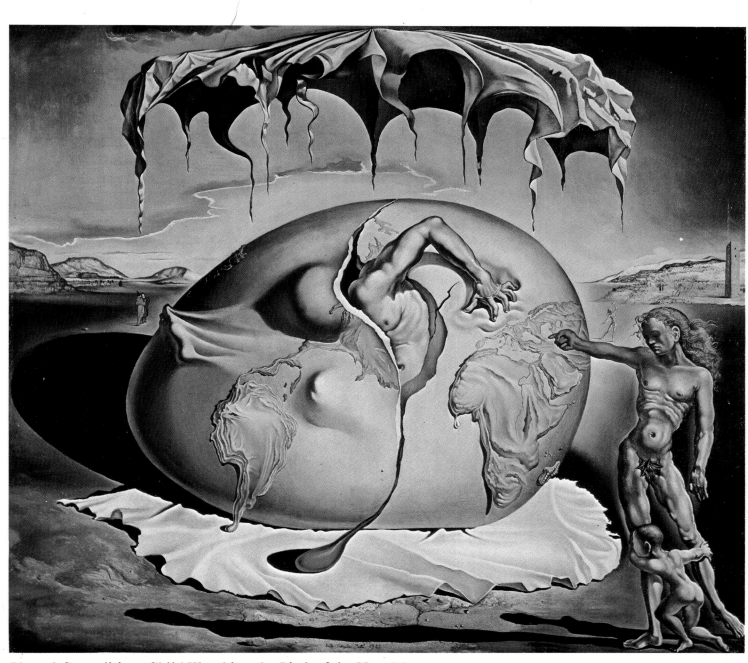

Plate 48 **Geopoliticus Child Watching the Birth of the New Man**

Plate 49
Apotheosis of Homer
1945
Oil on canvas
25¼ × 47 in (64 × 119 cm)
Staatsgalerie Moderner Kunst,
Munich

Dali has now become fascinated
with themes of Christianity as well
as discoveries in physics. About this
work he has merely said, 'Detailed
narration of the world of the blind'.
The work was to signify the end of
his Surrealist career.

television kill imagination and the spirit of man. Why were people
so incapable of fantasy? Why, for instance, didn't manufacturers of
toilets hide a bomb in the flush, to detonate when politicians pulled
the cord? Why, when ordering lobster, didn't one get a cooked
telephone? Dali's hatred of mass-production led him to consider an
automobile in the absurd act of gestation, as in *Debris of an Automobile
giving Birth to a Blind Horse biting a Telephone*.

At some point during Dali's stay in England, he discovered the
paintings of the Pre-Raphaelite Brotherhood, in whose works he
found 'paranoiac' evidence. Their very literary subject matter and
highly elaborated symbolism, combined with an obsessional attention
to detail, were all qualities that appealed to Dali's own predilection.
When he wrote 'Le surréalisme spectral de l'éternal féminin pré-
raphaelite' ('The spectral surrealism of eternal Pre-Raphaelite
femininity'), it was not an attempt to justify the movement aesthe-
tically, but to explore the hidden meaning behind the outward
appearance. Breton had made clear the Surrealist's distrust of art
criticism. He saw it as 'a complete failure' because the critic describes

Plate 50 *overleaf*
The Madonna of Port Lligat
1950
Oil on canvas
$56\frac{5}{8} \times 37\frac{3}{4}$ in (144 × 96 cm)
Lady Beaverbrook Collection,
Canada

Dali's preoccupation with a more
conscious objectivity and also
Roman Catholicism were the inspiration for the iconography of
this work, about which he has said:
'The weaning of food-furniture
made sacred: instead of a hole in
my nurse's back, a tabernacle con-
taining the divine bread open in the
body of Jesus.'

Plate 51 *overleaf*
Christ of St John of the Cross
1951
Oil on canvas
$90\frac{5}{8} \times 45\frac{5}{8}$ in (230 × 103 cm)
Glasgow Art Gallery

the form rather than the content. The true value of any work was its
ability, not to represent, but to prefigure. Breton suggested the
search for a new beauty that would be acceptable to our time. 'Beauty
will be convulsive,'[1] he insisted, and expressed his complete lack of
interest in works of art that did not produce 'a state of physical
disturbance characterised by the sensation of a wind brushing across
my forehead and causing me to really shiver', a sensation he relates
to erotic pleasure. Dali's paranoiac method, extended to his writings,
contributed in no small measure to the revelatory nature of that which
exists beneath the surface reality.

Unlike his other literary ventures into the significance of Millet's
Angelus, the legend of William Tell and Art Nouveau, Dali's art
showed no visual evidence of his meditations on the Pre-Raphaelites.
Possibly he merely wished to illustrate his enthusiasm for all that ran
counter to the prevailing fashion of the times and the appeal to 'the
bad taste of the age' that Breton spoke of. It was not until 1944, in
the painting *Tristan as Christ*, that Dali seems to have been partially
inspired by Burne-Jones, in the detail of the jewelled breastplate,

[1]'Beauty will be Convulsive', published
in *What is Surrealism?*, translated by
David Gascoyne, Faber & Faber,
London, 1936.

Plate 50 **The Madonna of Port Lligat**

Plate 51 **Christ of St John of the Cross**

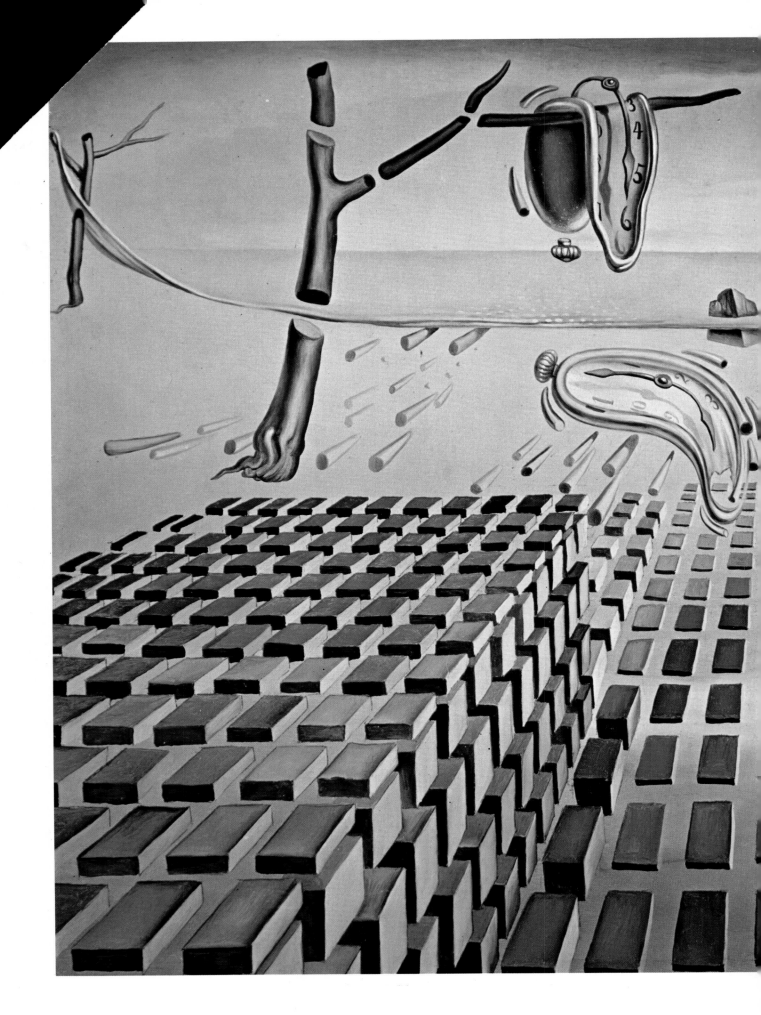

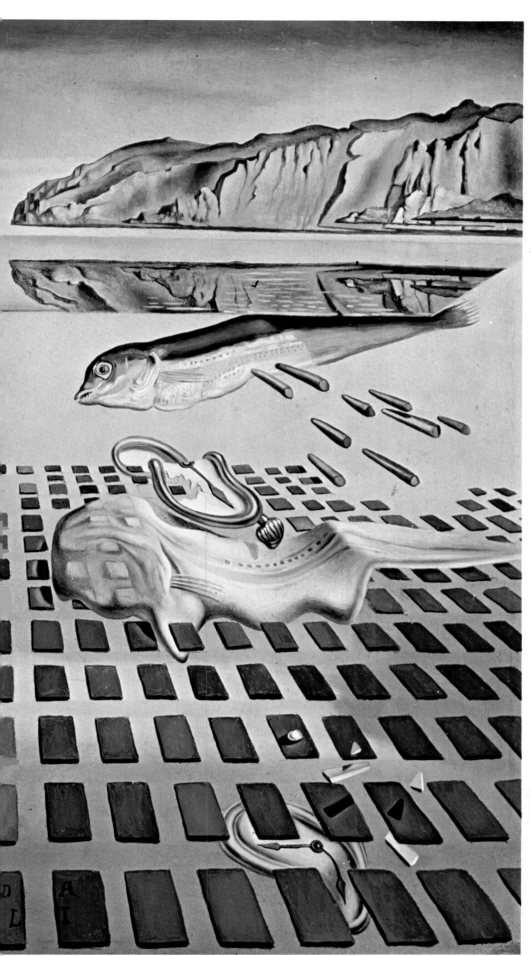

Plate 52
The Disintegration of the Persistence of Memory
1952–54
Oil on canvas
10 × 13 in (25.5 × 33 cm)
Collection of Mr and Mrs
A. Reynolds Morse, Salvador Dali
Museum, Cleveland (Ohio)

The full title of this work is *The Chromosome of a Highly Coloured Fish's Eye Starting the Harmonious Disintegration of the Persistence of Memory*. A number of compositional changes have been introduced into this work which is based on the 1931 *Persistence of Memory* (plate 14). The watch covered in ants has disappeared. The surface of the sea, sheet-like, hangs from the branch of a tree, and a fish now lies on what was a deserted beach.

'After twenty years of complete immobility,' said Dali, 'the soft watches disintegrate dynamically...'

Plate 53
**Young Virgin Autosodomised
by her own Chastity**
1954
Oil on canvas
16 × 12 in (40.5 × 30.5 cm)
Selected by Hugh Hefner for the
Playboy Collection.

About this painting Dali has said
'The horn of the rhinoceros, the
former uniceros, is in fact the horn
of the legendary unicorn, symbol of
chastity. The young virgin can lean
on it and play with it morally as was
practised in the time of courtly
love.'

the semi-transparent veil and preposterous pose of the figure that
only revealed the dubious nature of his growing academicism.

Between 1937 and 1939, Dali made three visits to Italy. Rome,
'Catholic in essence and in substance', he found was being destroyed
under Mussolini's modernisation, architecturally conceived 'by the
brain of one of those lamentable organisers of international expo-
sitions'. He joined Edward James at Amalfi, where he found inspiration for his Wagnerian ballet and spent two months on *Impressions of Africa* (plate 44) in which the treatment owes more to Velásquez than to any Italian master. The Munich crisis of 1938 prompted
a move to Monte Carlo and another painting, *The Enigma of Hitler*,
based on dreams brought on by the events of Munich. This picture
appeared to him 'to be charged with a prophetic value, as announcing
the medieval period which was going to spread its shadow over
Europe'. Chamberlain's umbrella appeared in this painting in a
sinister aspect, identified with the bat, and 'affected me as extremely
anguishing at the very time I was painting it ...'

In 1939 he made a second journey to America for his exhibition at
the Julien Levy Gallery. New York, 'an immense Gothic Rocquefort
cheese', was already familiar with this Paris Surrealist. His two
previous exhibitions, lectures at the Museum of Modern Art, as well
as the illustrations of the city made for the *American Weekly* in a
four-page spread, left little doubt of his growing popularity with the
American public. *Time* magazine put him on the cover, and Dali
images soon appeared everywhere. The Fifth Avenue store of Bonwit-
Teller invited him to make a window display. The theme was to be
Night and Day. Night was symbolised by a bed with a canopy of a
buffalo clutching a bloody pigeon in its mouth. The legs of the bed
were the four feet of the animal. Black bedsheets were covered with
burn marks, and a wax mannequin of the 1900 vintage, covered in
dust and cobwebs, lay across the bed with her head resting on artificial
live coals. Day showed another mannequin climbing into an ermine-
lined bath filled with water, while a pair of wax arms held a mirror
before her. Flowers grew out of the floor and surrounding furniture.
The following day Dali discovered that the decor had been altered;
his wax mannequins replaced by conventional ones and the bed
removed. Furious at the treatment, Dali entered the display window
and tried to upturn the bath of water in protest, only to slip and project
the tub through the plate glass window into the watching crowd
outside. Arrested by the police, he was brought before a night-court
and given a suspended sentence.

No less disastrous from Dali's point of view was his sideshow for the
New York World's Fair, to be called 'Dali's Dream of Venus'. He
soon discovered that all the corporation wanted was his name,
completely ignoring his ideas. Thoroughly disgusted, he sat down and
wrote a manifesto, *Declaration of Independence of the Imagination and
of the Rights of Man to his own Madness*. Before the 'Dream' was
finished he left for France. The means Dali cynically used to publi-

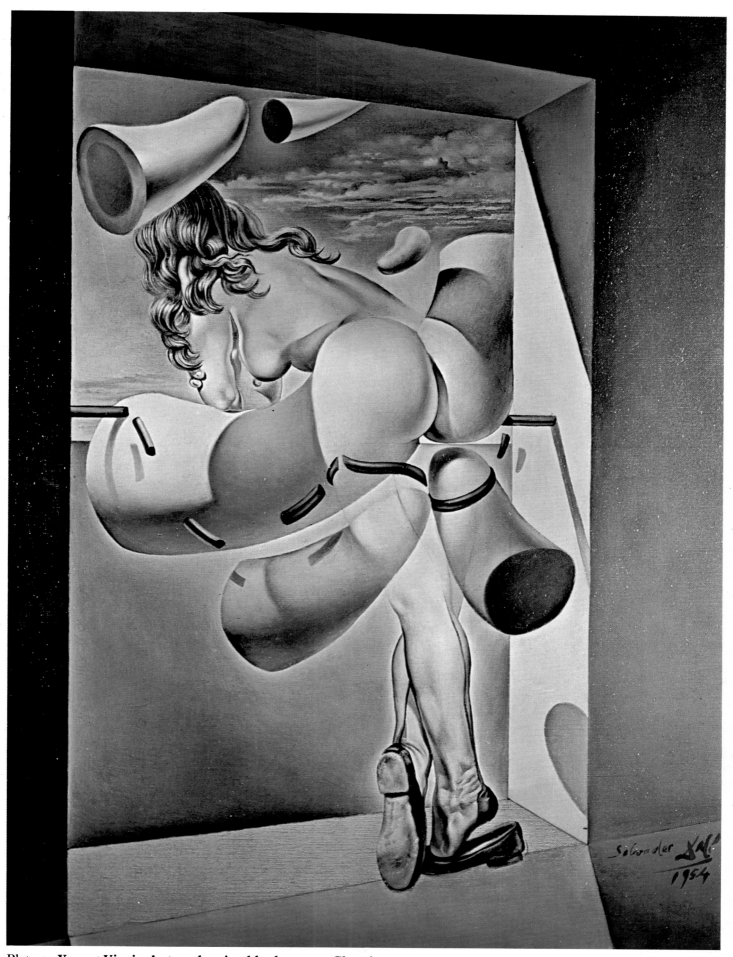

Plate 53 **Young Virgin Autosodomised by her own Chastity**

Plate 54
The Sacrament of the Last Supper
1955
Oil on canvas
$65\frac{3}{4} \times 105\frac{1}{2}$ in (167 × 268 cm)
Chester Dale Collection, National Gallery of Art, Washington (D.C.)

Dali based this work on the number 12: 12 hours of the day, 12 months of the year, 12 pentagons of the dodecahedron, 12 signs of the Zodiac, 12 Apostles around Christ.
'The Communion must be symmetrical,' he insisted.

cise himself, the endorsement of Franco in Spain and the growing academicism of his work had not passed unnoticed by the Surrealists, who rightly considered that he was bringing discredit to the ideas of Surrealism. This time the decision was unanimous: he was to be completely ignored by the movement. Dali had always insisted that he took Surrealism literally, neglected nothing to become the 'integral Surrealist' of which the logical outcome was his 'paranoiac-critical activity'. With equal determination he intended to 'become its leader as soon as possible', and to pass for the only authentic Surrealist. It was an attitude least calculated to identify him with a movement that had, since its inception, proclaimed a community of aims and had no wish to see Surrealism diminished by a wholehearted endorsement of his reactionary technique.

The advent of war brought a temporary truce to the Dali affair. After immense difficulties, some of the French Surrealists succeeded in reaching America. Man Ray and Nicholas Calas had arrived earlier and were soon joined by Tanguy, Masson, Matta, Duchamp, Seligmann and Breton. After moving to Spain, then Lisbon, Dali and Gala reached New York with the help of their friend, Caresse Crosby.[1] Recovering from their adventures at the country home of the Crosbys, Dali began writing his autobiography, widening his aesthetic interests and strengthening the ties with the Italian tradition. The Divine Proportion or, as Plato called it, the 'Golden Section' now received his attention, a principle he incorporated in the *Family of Marsupial Centaurs*, with its rigid diagonals dividing the composition into four equal triangles. Here Dali's hand is fully engaged by his conscious mind to achieve the Platonic ideal. It was to mark his reaction against the eloquence of his earlier works, in which revelation and discovery was the profound aim, and in which his masterly technique was used as a means and not as an end.

A return to classicism demanded a more conscious objectivity and a study of the pictorial science of the Renaissance. Geometry, mathematics, anatomy and perspective now received the same fanatical enthusiasm that earlier he had reserved for the interrogation of the unconscious as a springboard for inspiration. Both *Leda* and *Madonna and Child* are based on the Pythagorean pentagram, while the golden rectangle dominates *The Sacrament of the Last Supper* (plate 54). For Dali it meant 'integration, synthesis, cosmogony, faith'. His past he rejected as 'fragmentation, experimentation, scepticism'. With it all came an increased belief in the Catholic hierarchy and monarchy. Not surprisingly, therefore, we find him seeking the Pope's approval of one of his paintings. His hope for the future was clearly stated: 'a religious renaissance based on a progressive form of Catholicism'. Despite such views, and there are many on the subject, he believed he was the only true Surrealist. By such mental gymnastics did he seek to integrate Surrealism into the very aesthetic continuum which it has always set out to destroy.

During those war years in America, his flair for showmanship and publicity stunts, always good for newspaper headlines, made him a

[1]Caresse Crosby's autobiography, *The Passionate Years* (Dial Press, New York, 1953), gives a vivid account of this period.

Plate 54 **The Sacrament of the Last Supper**

Plate 55
**Galacidalacidesoxyribonu-
cleicacid**
1963
Oil on canvas
122 × 164 in (310.5 × 416.5 cm)
New England Merchants National
Bank, Boston (Massachusetts)

The molecular structures that were
to appear in a number of works of
this period are in this case those of
deoxyribonucleic acid.

[1] *The Case of Salvador Dali.*

household name to millions, who confused his money-making clown-
ing with Surrealism. It has accounted for his refusal to separate
painting from many minor arts and other aspects of aesthetics. During
the early 1940s he painted many portraits of the rich and famous, and
it was probably his long association with Jack Warner, the Hollywood
producer, in the five years it took to complete his portrait that led to
Dali's revived interest in the film as a medium of expression. Hitch-
cock's *Spellbound* and *The House of Mr Edwards* both had dream
sequences by Dali. Not yet realised is his own *The Wheelbarrow of
Flesh*, quoted by Fleur Cowles,[1] in which a paranoic woman falls
in love with a wheelbarrow. It contains such scenes as swans stuffed
with explosives blowing up, rhinoceroses climbing into the Trevi
fountain, hundreds of priests on bicycles carrying posters of Malen-
kov, and a shaven-headed woman, balancing an omelette on her head,
standing in the middle of a lake. He has written the book, designed
scenery and costumes for two ballets, designed jewellery in collaboration with the Duke di Verdura, and, next to paintings, has devoted
considerable time to writing well over thirty books. His widespread
activity has also touched on advertising, creating fashions for Chanel
and Schiaparelli, and lecture tours to many cities in the United States.

In the meantime, the Surrealists in New York were establishing their presence. Under the editorship of Charles Henri Ford, the bulletin *View* devoted a number of issues to Surrealism, one of which included an attack on Dali by Nicholas Calas called 'I say his flies are ersatz'.[1] In 1942 they started their own review, *VVV*, and the influence was beginning to have an effect on the intellectual life in the States. Dali was to remain isolated from the group's activity, who now referred to him as 'Avida Dollars' ('greedy dollars'), an anagram coined by Breton, or chose only to reproduce one of his advertisements made for Schiaparelli stockings. Unperturbed, Dali continued his own career as a 'completely deviant Surrealist' and set about cornering the religious market. The galactic forms revealed in the whorls of cauliflowers and the nuclear mysticism in the spiral of the rhinoceros horn were now given significance in his new works. In 1947 the Loew-Lewin film company organised a competition for a painting of *The Temptation of St Anthony* to be used in their film *The Private Affairs of Bel Ami*. From the eleven works submitted, five of which were by Surrealists, the jury chose the Max Ernst. Dali's contribution, which was less conventional, was quite the most

Plate 56
Divine Figures in the Wild Landscape of Cape Creus
1970
Oil on copper
Private collection.

[1]'Anti-Surrealist Dali', *View* No. 6, New York, 1941.

Plate 56 **Divine Figures of the Wild Landscape of Cape Creus**

Plate 57 **Nude (Desnudo de Calcomania)**

Plate 57
Nude (Desnudo de Calcomania)
1970
Various elements on card
Private collection
Never previously published.

Plate 58
The Shepherd and the Siren
1974
Hologram
Collection Enrique Sabater

outstanding. He wrote about it: 'the hermit sees in the clouds the paranoiac hallucinations of his temptation. The elephants carry on their backs erotic fountains, obelisks, churches, escurials. Elephants stride on almost invisible legs of spiders of desire. With outstretched arm, the saint bears his cross to exorcise the vision.' More revealing are the complex feelings that the picture betrays when one considers how ineffectual the cross appears to be against the advancing horde.

It is during Dali's Classical period that we find him fluctuating both in purpose and in style. The liaison between Freud and Roman Catholicism proposed a new reality, dependent in part on a laborious reconstruction of the past and the incongruities communicated from the subconscious. At the same time, conspicuous technical changes were to become noticeable in Dali's art, characterised by a more romantic handling of colour and a softening of forms that previously had been sharply defined. Also it was abundantly clear that he had no intention of relinquishing his personal symbols, which too often make their appearance in quite unlikely works. These early images once had significance but now become something of a mannerism.

Plate 59
Baisantje Empordanes
1978
Oil on copper
Collection Enrique Sabater

Dali's long interest in the Mannerist and Baroque traditions is noticeable in this painting, with its love of impasto and frenzied brushwork.

Since 1950 Dali has continued to extend his new mysticism, which was to pass through a number of phases and cover a variety of influences. His mental and plastic resources were brought to bear on the automatism of Abstract Expressionism, and he experimented with shooting lead bullets filled with ink at a lithographic stone for his illustrations to *Don Quixote*. Molecular structures give a new spatial dimension to paintings like *Tuna Fishing*, *The Ascension of St Cecilia* and *Galacidalacidesoxyribonucleicacid* (plate 55). At the same time, he launched as 'the saviour of modern painting' the concept of

a cosmic Dali,[1] painting rationally his re-found reality.

For half the year, Dali now retires to his beloved Port Lligat in Spain, where he lives like an ascetic, drawing strength from the isolation and peace of the surroundings. For, as he assures us, 'it is difficult to hold the world's interest for more than half an hour at a time. I myself have done so successfully every day for twenty years.' But that was written in 1958, and there is little evidence to suggest that the 'outboard motor continually running', as Picasso described him, is running out of energy.

[1]*Dali by Dali,* Harry N. Abrams Inc., New York, 1970.

chronology

1904   Born 11th May in Figueras, Gerona, Catalonia, Spain.

1914–18   Educated at the Academy of the Brothers of the Marist Order of Figueras.

1918–19   Experimented with Impressionism under the influence of Ramón Pitchot.

1920   Influenced by the Italian Futurists after seeing catalogues and manifestoes brought by his parents from Paris.

1921   Became a pupil at the School of Painting, Sculpture and Drawing in Madrid. Met Luis Buñuel, García Lorca and Pedro Garfias. Discovered Cubism through Juan Gris.

1922   Exhibited paintings at the Dalmau Gallery, Barcelona, with other students' work.

1923   Rejected Cubism and adopted the tenets of the 'Metaphysical School' of paintings which, under the guidance of Giorgio de Chirico and Carlo Carrà, explored the world of inner perception and experience. Suspended for a year from the School for rebellion.

1924   Imprisoned in Gerona for supposed political activity. Illustrated *Les Bruixes de Llers* by Fages de Climent.

1925   Returned to the School in Madrid. First one-man exhibition, Dalmau Gallery, Barcelona. Permanent expulsion from School.

1926–27   Contributed to *Gaseta de les Arts*, Barcelona. Received considerable praise from local art critics. Second one-man show at Dalmau Gallery. Influenced by Cubism and Picasso. Contributed to the journal *L'amic des Arts*.

1927   First visit to Paris. Met Picasso. Painted *Apparatus and Hand* (plate 5).

1927   Second visit to Paris. Miró introduced him to André Breton, Paul Eluard and other Surrealists. Painted *Anna Maria* and *Seated Girl*, shown in Barcelona. Later they were exhibited at the Carnegie Institute in Pittsburg. The first Dali paintings to be shown in America.

1928   Breton, Gala, Paul Eluard and Magritte visited Dali at Cadaqués. His painting now influenced by Ernst and Miró. Produced a group of mixed-media collages.

1929	Painted *Illumined Pleasures* (plate 9), *The Lugubrious Game* (plate 6) and other truly Surrealist works. Joined the Surrealist Group in Paris. First showing of the film *Un Chien Andalou* for which Dali and Buñuel wrote the scenario. In October married Gala.
1929–30	Came under the influence of Art Nouveau and the architecture of Gaudí. Rediscovered de Chirico of the early period (plate 19) as well as the 16th-century fantasies of Arcimboldo (plate 41). Wrote and illustrated *The Visible Woman*, which explained his 'paranoiac-critical method'. Illustrated *The Immaculate Conception* by André Breton and Paul Eluard. Collaborated with Buñuel on the film *The Golden Age* (plate 12), shown in the same year at Studio 28, Paris. In the ensuing riots paintings by Ernst, Miró, Dali, Tanguy and Man Ray were destroyed.
1930–33	Many contributions to the periodical *Surrealism in the Service of the Revolution*. Applied his paranoiac method to the legend of William Tell (plate 23), and the use of the double image in many paintings. Fascinated by Vermeer's *The Artist in his Studio*.
1930–38	Illustrated the second manifesto of Surrealism, *Le Revolver à Cheveux Blancs* by Breton, *Grains et Issues* by Tristan Tzara, *Cours Natural* by Paul Eluard, *Les Chants de Maldoror* by Isadore Ducasse (Comte de Lautréamont). Published an album of six photographs of paintings.
1931–32	Paintings and drawings included in 'The Newer Super-Realism' exhibition at the Wadsworth Atheneum, Hartford, Connecticut. Wrote *L'Amour et la Memoire* and *Babaouo* which included an essay on William Tell and a critique on the cinema. Exhibited at Julien Levy Gallery, New York.
1933	First one-man show, Julien Levy Gallery. Wrote on Millet's *Angelus* in *Minotaure*.
1934	First one-man show in London (Zwemmer Gallery). The Surrealists growing more concerned about his political expressions. Praise of Hitler and monarchist leanings led to official reprimand from Group; no longer attended the Surrealists' meetings. First visit to America. Illustrations of New York in the *American Weekly*.
1934–37	Series of paintings influenced by the effect of light on the beach at Rosas. Hitler, Lenin, *The Angelus* and telephones influence his iconography.
1935	Wrote *The Conquest of the Irrational*, defining his 'paranoiac-critical activity', and attacking abstract art.
1936	Exhibited in the International Surrealist Exhibition in London. Friendship with the English collector, Edward James, who formed the most representative collection of Dali's early work.

1937	Wrote *The Metamorphosis of Narcissus* illustrating his double-image painting of the same name (plate 36). First of three visits to Italy. Influenced by Palladio as well as Renaissance and Baroque paintings.
1938	Through Stefan Zweig and Edward James met Sigmund Freud in London. Made a portrait of him on blotting paper.
1939	Created a Surrealist window for Bonwit-Teller in New York. Arrested for smashing the window. Created 'The Dream of Venus' side show for the New York World's Fair. Published *Declaration of the Independence of the Imagination and of the Rights of Man to his own Madness*. Presentation of his ballet *Bacchanale*, with scenario and scenery by Dali.
1940	Left France for Spain at the beginning of the war. Moved to the United States where he remained until 1948. Lived in California.
1941–42	Major retrospective exhibition, Museum of Modern Art. Shown in eight cities. Established his reputation in the U.S.A. Created sets for the ballets *Labyrinth*, *El Cafe de Chinitas* and *Sentimental Colloquy*. Wrote his autobiography *The Secret Life of Salvador Dali* (Dial Press, New York). Began to paint portraits.
1943	Exhibition at Knoedler Gallery, New York. Completed studies for murals for the home of Helena Rubinstein. Wrote his novel *Hidden Faces* (Dial Press). Illustrations for *The Maze* by Maurice Sandoz; *Essays of Michel de Montaigne*, *As you like it* and *The Autobiography of Benvenuto Cellini*.
1948	Returned to Port Lligat, Spain. Became Classical. Illustrated *50 Secrets of Magic Craftsmanship*.
1949	Made his first religious paintings. *The Madonna of Port Lligat* (plate 50) was sanctioned by the Pope.
1951–52	Illustrations for Dante's *Divine Comedy*. Lectures on 'nuclear mystical' art. Painted *Christ of St John of the Cross* (plate 51). Wrote *Manifesto Mystique* which attempts to explain his mysticism.
1954–55	Published *Dali's Moustache* with Philippe Halsman. Retrospective in Rome. Painted *Corpus Hypercubicus* and *The Last Supper* (plate 54).
1956–59	Dali retrospective at Knokke Le Zoute, Belgium. Wrote *The Cuckolds of Modern Art*. Painted *Santiago El Grande*, now in Beaverbrook Art Gallery, Canada. First historical painting *The Discovery of America*. Wrote *Dali on Modern Art* (Dial Press, New York).
1961–63	New edition of *The Secret Life of Salvador Dali*. *Ballet de Gala* and Scarlatti's opera, *The Spanish Lady and the Roman Cavalier*, with sets and costumes by Dali. Religious painting *The Ecumenical Council* completed, also *The Battle of Tetuan* and *Galacidalacidesoxyribonucleicacid* (plate 55,

1963). Published *The Tragic Myth of the 'Angelus' of Millet* (Jean-Jacques Pauvert, Editeur, Paris).

1964–65 Major exhibition in Tokyo. Wrote *Journal of a Genius*, published in Paris (abridged edition, 1965, Doubleday, New York). Illustrations for the Bible. Began producing 'three-dimensional art' and the *Bust of Dante* sculpture.

1966–73 Alain Bosquet's *Conversations with Dali* (Editions Pierre Belfond. English translation, 1969, E. P. Dutton & Co. Inc., New York). Illustrated a de-luxe edition of *Alice in Wonderland* published by Random House, 1969. Harry N. Abrams Inc., New York, publish *Dali by Dali* with illustrations chosen by the artist and grouped under separate headings – the planetarian, the molecular, the monarchical, the hallucinogenic and the futuristic Dali.

1973 The Dali Museum opened at his birthplace Figueras.

1974 Completed the hologram *The Shepherd and the Siren* for Enrique Sabater. It includes a rare portrait of Gala.

1976 *The Unspeakable Confessions of Salvador Dali* published.

1978 First public showing, in the Teatro Museo Dali in Figueras, of *Babaouo*, a film based on the book first written in 1932.

bibliography

Barr, Alfred H. Jr, (editor) and Georges Hugnet, *Fantastic Art, Dada, Surrealism*, Museum of Modern Art, New York, 1937

Bosquet, Alain, *Conversations with Dali*, E. P. Dutton & Co. Inc., New York, 1969

Breton, André, *What is Surrealism?*, Faber & Faber, London, 1936. Includes the Introduction to the catalogue of Dali exhibition, Galerie Goemans, Paris, 1929.

Calas, Nicholas, 'Anti-Surrealist Dali: I say his flies are ersatz', *View*, New York, 1941

Cardinal, Roger, and Robert Stuart Short, *Surrealism, Permanent Revelation*, Dutton Pictureback, Studio Vista, London, 1970

Cowles, Fleur, *The Case of Salvador Dali*, Heinemann, London, 1959

Dali by Dali, Abrams, New York, 1970

Dauriac, J. P. *Les Diners de Gala*, Graphis 30. No. 172–152–9. 1974–75

Descharnes, R., *World of Salvador Dali*, Macmillan, 1972

Gascoyne, David, *A Short Survey of Surrealism*, Cobden-Sanderson, London, 1936

Gaunt, William, *Art's Nightmare : the Surrealist Paintings of Salvador Dali*, Studio, London, 1939

Dali, Salvador, *Diary of a Genius*, Hutchinson and New York, 1966

Gerard, Max, *Dali*, London and New York, 1968

Gerard, Max, *Dali-Dali-Dali*, Abrams, New York, 1974

Jean, Marcel, with the collaboration of Arpad Mezei, *The History of Surrealist Painting*, English translation by Simon Watson Taylor, Weidenfeld & Nicolson, London, 1960

Longstreet, Stephen (editor), *Drawings of Dali*, Borden, Los Angeles, 1964

Matthews, J. H., *An Introduction to Surrealism*, Pennsylvania State University Press, 1965

Morse, A. Reynolds, *Salvador Dali 1910–1965*, New York Graphic, 1965

Parrinaud, André, *Unspeakable Confessions of Salvador Dali*, W. H. Allen, 1976

Pierre, José, *Surrealism*, translated from the French by Paul Eve, Heron Books, London, 1970

Read, Herbert (editor), *Surrealism*, Faber & Faber, London, 1936 (paperback edition 1971)

Rubin, William, S., *Dada, Surrealism and Their Heritage*, Museum of Modern Art, New York, 1968

Salvador Dali, exhibition catalogue, Julien Levy Gallery, New York, 1941

Soby, James Thrall, *After Picasso*, Dodd Mead, New York, 1935

Soby, James Thrall, *Salvador Dali*, Museum of Modern Art, New York, 1941

Waldberg, Patrick, *Surrealism*, Thames & Hudson, London, 1965

Waldberg, Patrick, *The Initiators of Surrealism*, Collins in association with UNESCO, London, 1970

acknowledgments

The photographs in this publication were supplied by the owners of the paintings with the following exceptions:

Harry Abrams Inc., New York page 16 top; Joachim Blauel, Munich page 74; British Film Institue, London page 21; Camera Press Ltd, London – Robert Whitaker endpapers, title page right; A. C. Cooper Ltd, London (photographers of the Salvador Dali paintings:– the Edward James & New Trebizond Foundations); DASA Edicones SA, Barcelona back jacket, title page left, 10, 42, 85, 86, 87, 88–9; Roger Jean St Galat, Paris page 68; Photographie Giraudon, Paris page 22; Hamlyn Group Picture Library, London page 58; Hanz Hinz, Basle page 7; Lerner Photography Inc., New York (photographers of the Salvador Dali paintings:– The Mrs & Mrs Reynolds Morse Collection, Salvador Dali Museum, Cleveland, Ohio, and those paintings on pages 11, 12, 19, 30 and 43); Photo Meyer, Vienna page 62.

index

The figures in italic type refer to the captions to the plates.

KIANA'S
....
Body Sculpting

Kiana Tom

with

Jim Rosenthal

KIANA'S
Body Sculpting

Chapter-opening Photographs by
Dominic Petruzzi

Workout Photographs by
Robert Reiff

St. Martin's Press
New York

Library of Congress Cataloging-in-Publication Data

Tom, Kiana.
    Kiana's body sculpting / Kiana Tom, with Jim Rosenthal.
      p. cm.
    ISBN 0-312-11570-9
    1. Physical fitness for women.   2. Exercise for women.
  I. Rosenthal, Jim.   II. Title.   III. Title: Body sculpting.
  GV482. T65   1994
  613.7'045—dc20   94-25671
                                                          CIP

First Edition: January 1995
10 9 8 7 6 5 4 3

To Jim Rosenthal

Contents

Acknowledgments

I would like to thank so many important people in my life who have helped me achieve my goal in writing this book.

First and foremost, a big hug to my parents, who have given me their undivided support. They have taught me values, given me love and guidance and always been there for me. My parents made me who I am today. Mom, for your incredible energy, for being my role model and for your sound advice. You always made me see that I could "do whatever I put my mind to"—you were right. Dad, for your unconditional love. You have taught me to always do what is right, to be a leader and to strive for success. Mom and Dad, I love you!

I would like to thank all the people at St. Martin's Press, for all of their hard work and enthusiasm. A special *mahalo* (thank you in Hawaiian) goes out to the editor, George Witte, for initiating and coordinating the project. You're the best!

To Jim Rosenthal, my coauthor. You are a genius! A talented writer, editor and friend. Your enthusiasm and creativity have helped to make this book a success. You are one in a million, Jim!

Thank you to Robert Reiff and Dominic Petruzzi, two brilliant photographers. Thank you for all of your hard work!

Thank you to ESPN, the largest sports network, for the airtime, exposure and honor of being broadcast to the millions of viewers across the country, including the United States, Canada, Mexico, Brazil and Tokyo.

To the Sports Club Irvine, for the beautiful training facility to work out at, and for all of your support the past few years.

And to Flex, my super-hyperactive Dalmatian puppy. For your undying energy, without you I would never appreciate the word "relax."

And most of all, thanks to *you*, the millions of viewers across the world, for your support, your enthusiasm toward health and fitness, your letters and all of your kind words. *You are my true inspiration.*

—*Kiana Tom*

I'd like to dedicate this book to Diane for all her support and love. Thanks to George Witte, Robert Reiff, Shari Lesser Wenk and Scott and Elizabeth Bagish for their invaluable assistance.

A special thank you to Kiana, a pleasure to work with and a wonderful person to count on as a friend.

—*Jim Rosenthal*

KIANA'S
....
Body Sculpting

CHAPTER 1

Introduction to the

Body–Sculpting System

Before I launch into the exercise and diet system I've designed for you, one that will make great changes in the way you look and how you feel, I want to tell you a little something about my background.

I didn't just make a decision to get into the fitness business—the whole experience was an evolutionary process for me. I had many choices to make along the way: Would I opt for the sometimes bizarre world of female bodybuilding, or go the more mainstream—and healthy—route of female body sculpting? A tough decision, but one that would set the tone for my professional career and direct me on the road to success and satisfaction. First, let's put my career into some historical perspective.

I became involved with weight training before most people really knew what they were supposed to be doing in the gym, before it was popular to lift for aesthetics or sports performance. I guess you could say I was into experimentation, taking my body to the limit of its physical potential.

Initially, tennis was the sport that pushed me into being in top shape. I was only sixteen and ready to try anything that would help me improve my performance. My high school tennis coach encouraged me to lift weights to increase the power of my serve. My serve did improve, but there was one other intriguing fringe benefit that came from lifting weights: I started noticing some nice—and significant—changes in my appearance.

That's how it all got started. When I saw the added shape my body took on, the increased definition and muscle tone, I thought it was amazing that I could actually sculpt my body and increase my strength. I got pretty excited about the changes. It helped that my mom was a physical education teacher. She was always talking to me about body mechanics and physiology, and she supported my decision to lift consistently for health, fitness and aesthetics.

I was always inquisitive about everything when I was a teenager—in fact, I'm still pretty inquisitive. I'd go right up to the person with the best physique in the gym and I'd ask him (or her) what he did to look that way. Then I'd give that training strategy a try to see if it helped me; basically, I'd experiment with every training formula to hit upon the perfect system for working my body.

Then, while I was at UCLA, I started training at Gold's Gym in Venice, the mecca for bodybuilding in Southern California. I also trained at the Wooden Center (named for former UCLA basketball coach John Wooden) after classes.

I hate to admit it, but I was obsessed with my training. When I set my mind to something, it's all I think about. I would not leave the gym until I finished every set and repetition of every exercise on my large laundry list of things to do. It could be 11 P.M. and I still wouldn't stop. My friends could be waiting for me to go to a party and I'd tell them: "Hey, I have to finish one more set of calves." Pretty soon I met them at the party, though it was very late. That's how obsessed I was in those days. Yes, I was strict with my training regimen, but it was more of a mental commitment to fulfilling my physical potential.

That total commitment helped me build the strong training foundation. I still train hard, but I'm not obsessed with working out seven days a week until 11 P.M. It doesn't require as much work to maintain your physique as it does to build it from the ground up.

Let's face facts: Consistency allowed me to get into the shape I'm in now. It enabled me to achieve all my goals and land a part on the "BodyShaping" TV show on ESPN. But I'll admit that I took things too far. My friends at UCLA had to indulge all my little eccentricities—I was driving everybody crazy by bringing baked potatoes with me for casual drives around Westwood, eating nothing but low-fat, unprocessed foods, drinking nothing but bottled water without sodium. I was too one-dimensional.

I believe that women need to strike a balance in their lives. Balance breeds success. I don't think you can be happy while training eight hours a day. And that's one of the main reasons why I decided to stay away from female bodybuilding.

I'll tell you how I made this decision. I entered my first female bodybuilding show back in college—those obsessive UCLA days—and won easily. I was really excited about my success—even if it was just the Miss San Diego Border States Contest—and geared up for the next show.

But each time you win a contest, the judges bump you up to the next division. I competed in the Palm Springs Muscle Classic and snagged second place. Not bad. But I was beginning to come to an important realization: As I moved up the ladder with each show, the women kept getting progressively bigger and bigger. I'd see pictures of myself side-by-side with the other female bodybuilders and I looked skinny by comparison.

I was only nineteen, a sophomore in college, but I had an important decision to make: Did I want to get bigger so I could compete as a female bodybuilder? I was already 127 pounds, which is pretty heavy for me. Or did I want to stay muscular and lean yet still retain my femininity?

I decided to stick with what I liked—the lean, feminine and muscular look instead of the more masculine, muscle-bound image that the female bodybuilders convey.

Women should aspire to a sleek, toned and feminine appearance—like a work of classical art. Big shoulders and muscular backs don't work for me. Bigger is not better.

The key to success—regardless of your goals—is to make your workouts fun and inspiring. I've never had a problem with motivation because I love to work out and get my body into top shape. I've found that if you go to the gym—whether it's at the club or in your home—do the work and get it over with quickly and efficiently, you'll never be bored or burned out on training. The more you dwell on what you have to do, the less likely it is you'll get anything done. Just do it. Just enjoy it. Without pleasure, what's the point?

Now, with the body-sculpting system, working out can be fun and pleasurable. Most women can't afford the time to cultivate an obsession with training. The plan is to get in shape, to look better and feel healthier. Keep your body and mind stimulated by changing exercises around as much as possible. Try new exercises, vary the number of sets and reps, then have a partner train with you to push you to the next level. Join two different gyms so you don't get lulled into a monotonous pattern. New people and new environments are very stimulating.

The whole point of this system is that it's fun and interesting—it's the only way to stay consistent and see any progress. People give up on fitness because it becomes dull and self-defeating. Don't set unrealistic goals. Make the process as much fun as the satisfaction you get from making the gains. That's what the body-sculpting system is all about.

CHAPTER 2

Body Sculpting in Action

Women come in different shapes and sizes. And, yes, some women don't have to work as hard as others to get into shape, but if you're motivated and focused you can do it. However, even the most glamorous models are forced to combat the female trouble spots—those genetic problem areas that haunt a woman, especially as she ages.

Throughout the course of this book, I want you to think of me as your personal trainer and problem-solver. My approach to one-on-one training is completely analytical. Assess and evaluate. Some women, for instance, have thin legs and need to add size. Other women might have excess body fat and need to shape and tone their thighs. Most women are not looking for mass. Again, it's a matter of body sculpting versus bodybuilding; take what you've got and make it better according to your unique body type and genetics.

Let me show you body sculpting in action. We all know that men are prone to storing fat around their midsection. Love handles, of course, are another big concern. Women's big three hot spots are the triceps (the muscle that's located at the back of the upper arm), the thighs and the buttocks. In this chapter I will show you how to tone, tighten and shape these problem areas. My strength as a trainer is being able to study a woman's physique to determine what she needs to solve her problem.

Problem-solving is the name of the game. Here's my plan of attack for combatting five of the most common trouble spots for women. Designing a beautiful body is not as hard as you think.

Trouble Spot: Flabby Triceps. The aging process always works against you in the fight to banish unsightly fat. One of my clients is a thirty-eight-year-old woman, a working mother who took several years off from training. Not surprisingly, she was out of shape.

Now, I will never force a beginner to overtrain in search of a quick-fix solution. It's a gradual program of developing the targeted muscle through exercise and removing the excess fat through a careful, consistent diet. We'll talk more about nutrition in Chapter 7.

The odyssey begins slowly—just one triceps exercise, 2 to 3 sets, twice a week. We'll start with a simple movement like a triceps pressdown. With a palms-down grip, grasp the bar at a triceps-pressdown station. Slowly push the bar down, keeping your arms close to your sides and your elbows steady, for 2 to 3 sets of 8 to 10 repetitions. It's always just 2 to 3 sets per workout. Then, if you feel comfortable with that exercise, you can spice things up a bit by substituting either a two-arm dumbbell extension or a triceps kickback. But it's always just one exercise per workout, 2 or 3 sets of 8 to 10 reps. The goal is to begin with basic exercises that tone and shape the triceps without putting undue stress on the joints, tendons and ligaments.

The beginning phase lasts about four weeks. Once you have mastered proper form and can lift a heavier weight for 8 to 10 reps and understand the proper technique of the three basic movements, then go ahead to the intermediate triceps program and diversify your workout with a few more advanced exercises: lying triceps extensions with a barbell, triceps pressdowns with rope handle and close-grip bench presses are all good options. Pick two or three of these muscle toners and do them for 2 to 3 sets of 8 to 10 reps, two days per week. The weight stays fairly low, as the goal is to shape the muscle rather than to pack on mass. Most women do not want huge triceps; it's not a look that's particularly feminine or sexy.

Stay with the intermediate triceps program for at least six months. Check with a personal fitness trainer to monitor your progress. Don't try to do too much too soon. You might also want to consult with a fitness expert when you think you're ready to jump from the beginner to the intermediate level. Overtraining is the worst-case scenario for anyone trying to stay in top shape. You'll get injured, burned out, or both.

Advanced triceps training involves doing three or four exercises for 2 to 3 sets of 8 to 10 reps, two times per week. Now you're ready to hit the triceps from different angles. Start with a pushing movement like a triceps pressdown with rope handle, then go to kickbacks (using a much lighter weight), do your lying triceps extensions for some added muscle tone and finish with dips and two-arm dumbbell extensions to really isolate the muscle. Parallel bar dips are another great triceps toner—and you get a little chest development as a bonus.

Some of you—and this is true for me—may want to lift with a lighter weight in the 12 to 15 rep range; my triceps tend to get too big if I stay with a weight that allows me to knock out only 8 to 10 reps. Experiment with the weight and exercise selection to find the perfect program for your special needs.

The Triceps Program

*Beginner**

Exercise	Sets	Reps
Triceps pressdown	2–3	8–10
Triceps kickback	2–3	8–10
Two-arm dumbbell extension	2–3	8–10

Select one of the three exercises and perform twice per week.

*Intermediate**

Exercise	Sets	Reps
Triceps pressdown	2–3	8–10
Lying triceps extension	2–3	8–10
Triceps kickback	2–3	8–10
Triceps pressdown (with rope handle)	1	8–10
Two-arm dumbbell extension	1	8–10
Close-grip bench press	1	8–10

Select two or three exercises and perform twice per week.

*Advanced**

Exercise	Sets	Reps
Triceps pressdown (with rope handle)	3	8–10
Triceps kickback	3	8–10
Lying triceps extension	3	8–10
Two-arm dumbbell extension	3	8–10
Close-grip bench press	3	8–10
Dip	3	8–10

Select three or four exercises and perform twice per week.

Trouble Spot: Jiggly Thighs. Those pesky thighs—they're a recurring nightmare for many of my clients. Women always ask me if there's a surefire method of burning fat off the quadriceps (the four-headed muscle group on the upper thigh). The answer is yes, you don't have to live with cellulite. Don't panic. I'm going to help you put those jiggles to rest, once and for all. A low-fat diet and a consistent cardio schedule stay in force as part of your body-sculpting stratagem. Now let's turn to the specific weight-training tips used for slimming and toning.

Beginner: Start with a 10-minute warm-up on the stationary bike. This really helps to stimulate blood flow to the legs, limber up the muscles you'll be working and put that heart rate into its target zone (65 to 85 percent of your max heart rate).

Begin your exercises with the 45-degree leg press; it's a basic body shaper, ideal for toning the thighs. Do the first set with a very light weight for 20 reps. Slowly increase the weight until you're lifting in the 12 to 15 range for 2 more sets. That's all you have to do for the first four weeks. If you get bored, feel free to substitute leg extensions, lunges or hip adduction/abduction movements. Use the hamtractor machine, a toner for the hamstrings, as a nice complementary exercise to hit the legs from every angle.

Light weights and high reps are your bodysculpting tactics for toning thighs, as you'll sculpt sleek, sexy, shapely legs instead of packing on size.

After you're done with the weights, hop on the bike for at least twenty minutes to burn off the excess fat. Then hit the sauna or steam to unwind. This is a one-day-a-week ritual until you're ready to move on to the intermediate level.

Intermediate: It takes about four weeks to progress to this point. Repeat the cardio phase of the beginner's leg program, though you may want to add 10 minutes to your post-weight-workout aerobics. Do 2 sets each of leg extensions and finish off with a few sets of adductor/abductor exercises for your hips.

Advanced: Now it's time to add squats or Smith-machine squats to shape the outer thigh with a little extra lean muscle mass. Cardio intensity stays about the same. Take a good, hard look in the mirror to determine how much mass you want to pack on; keep the weight light and the reps high—muscle tone, not unwanted size, will be your reward.

The Thigh Program

Beginner*

Exercise	Sets	Reps
Leg press	3	20–15–12
Leg extension	3	12–15
Lunge	3	12–15
Hip adduction/ abduction	3	12–15

*Select one exercise, preferably the leg press, and perform once per week. Or you can do 1 set of each exercise for a total of 4 sets.

Intermediate*

Exercise	Sets	Reps
Leg press	3	12–15
Leg extension	3	12–15
Lunge	3	12–15
Hip adduction/ abduction	3	12–15

*Select two exercises and perform twice per week.

Advanced*

Exercise	Sets	Reps
Leg press	4	12–15
Leg extension	4	12–15
Lunge	4	12–15
Hip adduction/ abduction	4	12–15
Squat or Smith-machine squat	4	12–15

*Select three exercises and perform twice per week.

Trouble Spot: Calves. Most women ignore training their calves, as if the lower part of the leg didn't really exist. That's silly. Men do like to see women with shapely calves. And it doesn't take that much time or effort to put the body-sculpting principles to work for your lower leg muscles.

Only two exercises, two or three times per week, will do the trick. Keep the weight light and the reps high.

The Calf Program

Exercise	Sets	Reps
Standing or seated calf raise	2–3	12–15
Donkey calf raise machine	2–3	12–15

Trouble Spot: Sagging Buttocks. Aren't men lucky? They don't have to worry about their glutes showing the effects of gravity. I'm going to show you how to tone and shape your butt to resist the ravages of the aging process, to lift, shape and firm your bottom.

Squats place a lot of emphasis on your gluteal muscles. *Hyperextensions* (also known as back raises) strengthen the lower back while sculpting a nice round bottom. Here's how you do a hyperextension: Extend your upper body over the end of a high bench with your pelvis resting on the support pad. Lock your legs under the heel support. Place your hands behind your head and bend forward at the waist until your upper body is vertical to the floor. Raise your torso until it's slightly past parallel, feel the contraction in your lower back, and repeat for 2 sets of 12 to 15 repetitions. Lunging onto a step is an effective glute exercise. And leg presses with your feet up high on the platform will also work your butt. Vary the exercises; try to work your butt two or three times per week (with at least one of the aforementioned exercises).

The Buttocks Program

Exercise*	Sets	Reps
Squat	2	12–15
Leg press	2	12–15
Hyperextension	2	12–15
Lunge	2	12–15

*Pick one and perform two or three times per week.

Trouble Spot: Weak Midsection/Abdominals. Diet and cardiovascular exercise are just as important for a trim midsection as the abdominal movements.

Cardiovascular Exercise: Women need to balance resistance training with consistent fat-burning aerobics and a careful, low-fat diet (I'll give you the scoop on diet in Chapter 7). You can't spot-reduce; all the triceps exercises

in the world won't eliminate the fat; it took a while to put the extra fat on, and it will take a little time to burn it off. Be patient.

Here's a cardio program that is effective and realistic:

Phase 1 (Beginner) Nothing fancy; just get outside and walk for 20 to 30 minutes every day. Go at an easy pace. Be consistent.

Phase 2 (Intermediate and Advanced) Pump up the volume by working at 65 to 85 percent of your maximum heart rate *(220 minus your age equals your maximum heart rate)* for at least 20 minutes, four days a week. Twenty minutes is a turning point in your cardio program; before the 20-minute mark you're primarily burning glucose; after the 20-minute mark you're actually burning off your fat stores. What a relief!

Don't kill yourself in pursuit of shedding pounds. Vary your program and stay on a realistic schedule. I like to split up my indoor cardio workout this way:

10 minutes on the Versaclimber or stairclimber
10 minutes on the stationary bike
10 minutes on the treadmill

Keep your fat intake down to 10 to 15 percent of your daily total of calories. Work your way up to 45 minutes of aerobic exercise—remember, you only burn fat after the 20-minute mark. The longer you stay on that bike or treadmill, the better your chances of burning fat-based calories.

Okay, so you're eating less fat and working out on the bike with consistency. I like that. Now I'm going to ask you to go the extra mile for the sake of your waistline: Train your abdominal muscles every single day in a circuit, performing four different movements for 1 set, as many reps as you can handle.

Crunches, side crunches, V-ups and lying leg raises will tone your obliques, serratus and rectus abdominus—the three primary muscles of the midsection. Try to achieve 25 repetitions of three of these ab exercises without resting. Always begin with a simple ab stretch to loosen up the targeted muscles: Lie down on a mat and extend your arms out to the side. Bring both knees together and lift them over to your right and then to your left. Contract your abs as you go through the stretch. (See photo on page 55.) Start slowly with 5-and-10-rep sets; work your way up. Focus on exhaling on the contraction and inhaling as you stretch the muscle. Visualize a tight, shapely stomach. Ten

minutes a day is all it takes for a more feminine and beautiful body.

The Abdominal Program

Exercise	Sets*	Reps*
Crunch	1	Max
Side crunch	1	Max
V-up	1	Max
Lying leg raise	1	Max

*This is a circuit-training approach to ab training—do one exercise until failure, then immediately advance to another exercise until you can't pump out any more reps. Do this every day of the week to sculpt your midsection and build your endurance. The goal, again, is to reach 25 reps for at least three of the four exercises.

TROUBLE SPOT

Flabby Triceps

A

B

TRICEPS KICKBACK

Emphasis: *triceps* Grasp a dumbell in your right hand, placing your left hand on your left knee for support (*photo A*). With your right elbow bent and at your side, straighten your right arm behind you until it's parallel to the ground at shoulder height (*photo B*).

A

TWO-ARM DUMBBELL EXTENSION
Emphasis: *triceps* Grasp a relatively light dumbbell and raise it over your head with both arms extended (*photo A*). Lower the dumbbell behind your head (*photo B*), then straighten your arms for a full contraction.

B

A

B

TRICEPS PRESSDOWN
(with rope handle)

Emphasis: *triceps*

Grasp a rope handle attached to a pressdown station; your elbows are bent (*photo A*). Slowly press the handle down until your arms straighten out (*photo B*); keep your arms close to your sides and your elbows steady.

A

B

DIP
Emphasis:
triceps/lower
chest Hold your body
up at arm's length above the
bars of a dip station *(photo
A)*. Cross your feet over
each other so they don't
impede your movement.
Now lower yourself as far as
possible *(photo B)*, press
back up to the starting
position and flex your lower
chest muscles at the top.

A

CLOSE-GRIP BENCH PRESS

Emphasis:

triceps/chest Lie on a bench with a close grip—hands inside of shoulder-width—on the bar (*photo A*). Bring the bar up to arm's length over your chest (*photo B*), then lower it to your chest, focusing on the triceps as you lift and lower the bar.

B

A

LYING TRICEPS EXTENSION
Emphasis:
triceps Lie back with your head at the end of a flat bench; your arms have a palms-down grip on an E-Z curl bar and your arms are straight and directly over your chest (*photo A*). Lower the bar—by bending your elbows—down to your forehead to contract your triceps (*photo B*). Press the bar back up to the top, straightening your arms, and repeat.

B

TROUBLE SPOT

Jiggly Thighs

LEG EXTENSION
Emphasis:
quadriceps

Sit on a leg-extension machine, your feet tucked under the pads (*photo A*). Raise the weight until your legs are parallel to the floor (*photo B*). Lower and repeat.

A

B

A

B

SQUAT

Emphasis: *quadriceps, gluteals, lower back* Place a barbell across your upper back (*photo A*). With your head up and back straight, squat until your thighs are parallel to the floor (*photo B*). Return to the starting position—slowly—and repeat. This exercise can also be performed with dumbbells (*see* Chapter 4, Portable Workouts). Squats on an elevated surface—such as a weight plate— will put more emphasis on your thigh muscles, while squatting onto a flat surface puts more emphasis on your glutes.

A

LEG PRESS
Emphasis: *quadriceps*

Place your feet flat on the platform
of a leg-press machine (*photo A*).
Your legs should be straight, but your
knees should not be locked. Bend your
knees, bringing the weight as close
as possible to your chest (*photo B*)
Press the weight back up to the
starting position.

B

ABDUCTOR MACHINE

Emphasis: *outer thigh* Secure yourself on the outer-thigh (abductor) machine and push out. Don't arch your back; exhale on the contraction.

ADDUCTOR MACHINE

Emphasis: *inner thigh* The inner-thigh (adductor) machine is the opposite of the abductor: You push in on the pads; again, exhale on the contraction.

SMITH-MACHINE SQUAT

Emphasis:
*quadriceps,
gluteals,
lower back*

A more controlled
version of the standard
squat. With the bar
resting on your upper
back and balanced
on a Smith machine
(*photo A*), lower your
body until your thighs
are parallel to the floor
(*photo B*). Always grasp
the bar with your wrists
straight to ensure proper
alignment. Push up
(but don't bounce)
from your feet until
you reach the top.

A

B

A

B

LUNGE

Emphasis: *quadriceps and hamstrings*

With a dumbbell in each hand—head up, back straight (*photo A*)—step forward with your right leg (*photo B*) until your right thigh is parallel to the ground. Step back into the starting position and repeat with your left leg. *For a variation*: Lunge up onto a step, keeping your knee over the ankle, to work your glutes.

TROUBLE SPOT

Calves

A

DONKEY CALF RAISE

Emphasis: *gastrocnemius (the diamond-shaped muscle on the outside of your calf) and the soleus (inner calf)* Position your lower back beneath the donkey calf-raise machine's pad, the balls of your feet resting on the edge of the platform. Lower (*photo A*) and raise (*photo B*) your heels; repeat.

B

STANDING CALF RAISE

Emphasis:
gastrocnemius

Place the balls of your feet on a block. Raise (*photo A*) and lower your heels. Then turn your toes out (*photo B*) to enhance the width of your calves.

A

B

A

SEATED CALF RAISE

Emphasis: *soleus* Sitting at a calf-raise machine (*photo A*), place the balls of your feet on the toe block and set the pad across your knees. Raise your toes as high as you can (*photo B*) and then lower your heels as far as possible. Turn your toes out (*photo C*) to enhance the width of your calves.

B

C

TROUBLE SPOT

Weak Midsection/ Abdominals

A

B

LYING LEG RAISE

Emphasis: *lower abdominals* Lie on a flat bench with your hands under your butt, your lower back pressed into the bench and your head raised, with the chin up (*photo A*). Begin with your legs up and slowly lower them until they're just above bench level (*photo B*). Exhale at the bottom, then repeat.

A

B

V-UP *(beginner)*

Emphasis: *upper and lower abdominals* Sit on a bench sideways with your knees tucked in toward your chest and your hands behind you (palms down) for support (*photo A*). Bring your feet forward, extending your legs out in front of you as you contract your abs (*photo B*). Exhale on the contraction, then return to the starting position and repeat.

A

V-UP *(advanced)*

Emphasis: *lower abdominals* Begin with your legs straight out in front of you while seated sideways on a flat bench (*photo A*), then bring your legs up and crunch your abs so that your upper and lower body form a V (*photo B*).

B

Beginner

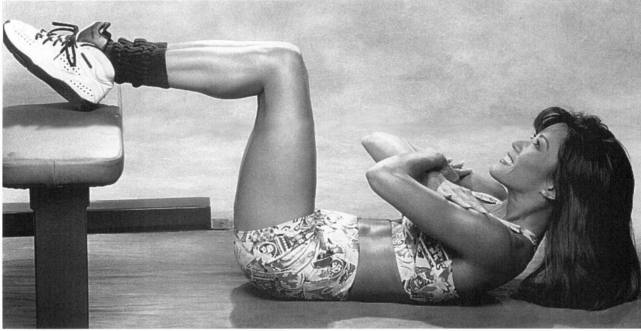

Intermediate

CRUNCH SEQUENCE
Emphasis: *upper abdominals*

Beginner: Lie on the floor or a mat, bend your knees and place your feet upon a flat bench in front of you. Extend your arms and crunch forward (bringing rib cage toward pelvis) in small pulses. Keep your chin up and lift your shoulders off the mat or floor.

Intermediate: Fold your arms over your chest and crunch forward. This cross-arm position increases the resistance slightly.

Advanced: Place your hands behind your head to add more resistance.

Most Advanced: Bring your arms all the way behind your head for the ultimate amount of resistance on your abs.

Crunch Variation #1: Emphasis: upper abs. Same as the advanced crunch, only this time you're lifting one of your knees to increase the resistance.

Crunch Variation #2: Emphasis: upper abs. Much like the beginner crunch, but raising one knee enhances the resistance.

Advanced

Most Advanced

Crunch Variation #1

Crunch Variation #2

AB STRETCH

This is an ideal warm-up to your abdominal workout. Lie down on a mat and extend your arms out to the side. Bring both knees together and lift them over to your right and then to your left (*as in photo*). Contract your abs as you go through the stretch.

CHAPTER 3

The 30-Minute (Beginner) Workout

In a perfect world you'd have all day and unlimited time to train toward achieving the perfect body. These days, though, you're lucky if you can get anything done at all to fulfill your goals. My 30-minute workout plan is designed for women who don't have enough time to train with my other body-sculpting programs.

This one simple workout mixes and matches the best, most effective exercises for each body part. Put it all together and you hit every major muscle group in 30 minutes. It's the bare minimum you can do to improve upon—or at the very least maintain—your level of lean body mass.

Okay, say you haven't trained at all before starting on this time-saving regimen. In that case, yes, you will gain some lean body mass.

But for those of you who are already on a program—whether it's the one we discussed in the previous chapter or something you've been faithful to for years—think of this as a one-month break from a more intensive workout.

Or you can do this if you're really tired but still want to slip in a quick conditioning, energizing fix. It's what I'll do if I don't have time to perform my regular exercise routine. It also works perfectly as a beginner program, one that will prepare you for the more advanced workouts in Chapters 2 and 6.

Here's how it works. I always pair a mass-building exercise with a shaping exercise for each body part. I'd never do two pressing movements—such as a bench press and a decline press for chest—as both exercises build the size of the muscle. I prefer to do my decline bench presses with dumbbells; it's much easier than using the bar: Lie on a decline bench and grasp two dumbbells, lifting them until they touch at arm's length above your chest. Lower the weight slowly until the dumbbells come down to your collarbone. Press back up to the top and repeat. I switch off between a press (for size) and a flye (for shape). That's the best way to get the most done in the least possible time.

One other trick of the trade is *supersetting*—moving from one exercise to another (either within the same body part or a different muscle group) with little or no rest between sets. Instead of pumping out three sets of bench presses in a row, for example, you'd move right from one set of bench presses to one set of flyes. You go back and forth until you've completed three sets of each exercise.

A note of caution before getting started: Always use a lighter weight when supersetting or you'll fatigue too quickly and you won't be able to finish your workout. There's also the added benefit of turning your weight routine into a mild aerobic session-cum-endurance test—a double whammy for your body.

The 30-minute workout is ideal for those of you just starting out on a fitness plan. You get the feel of the weight; you become familiar with many of the core movements that drive the body-sculpting system.

I like to put my new clients on this program just to see how they can handle the basic exercises. It's a great motivator because you can't waste any time—in and out of the gym in a flash, but with a good pump to show for the time invested.

The goal is to thwart any possible excuses to get out of training. How many times does your day get so out of control that you begin to question the sanity of squeezing in a workout?

Believe me, I can relate to that feeling. But this is what I do for a living. That's why I developed this quick and easy plan of action to take the place of just blowing it off for the day. Outsmart yourself; if you tend to get busy late in the day or in the evening, try to work out in the morning or at lunch.

Don't use this as the only workout you ever do. The 30-minute session is not a comprehensive approach to training. You do need the other exercises we discussed in the chapter on body sculpting to tackle those trouble spots that plague women of all ages. But this does add variety to your fitness regimen. It gets the blood flowing into the muscles, keeping your body prepared for the serious gains you'll enjoy with your regular workouts.

One of the secrets to my success is not taking too much time off between workouts. It's important to allow for enough rest to bounce back from strenuous training, but try not to take more than three days off in a row. You'll lose your momentum and your body will lose its sensitivity to the weights. With the 30-minute plan, you can sneak in a session in less than an hour—including a 10-minute cardiovascular pump on the stationary bike or treadmill and a quick shower.

THE 30-MINUTE PLAN OF ACTION

This easy-to-follow workout is a two-day-a-week commitment. Always start with the biggest muscle group—the legs kick things off. Begin by warming up on the treadmill or the stairmaster for 10 to 15 minutes to get your blood flowing and your heart rate up into its training zone (*220 minus your age equals your maximum heart rate*). Don't just start lifting without any warm-up or you'll put yourself at risk of an injury. I don't care how pressed for time you are—there's never any reason to get injured in the name of getting in shape. That's silly.

Save your stretching for after the workout. I know a lot of people will tell you to stretch before training with weights, but I prefer doing it following the conditioning regimen—it's a great cool-down for the muscles and helps to minimize post-workout soreness.

Legs: Begin with a set of leg extensions, 8 to 12 reps, and then get into the squats or leg presses, the heavy-duty mass builders. Beginners should start with 1 set of each exercise; intermediate trainers will want to do 2 or 3 sets; those of you who have been at it for a while can go for 4 sets. Stay in the 8 to 12 rep range on all of the exercises. Do leg extensions and squats on the first training day of the week, then switch to lunges and leg curls on Day 2. Flip-flop your exercises to keep your workouts fresh. Consult the chart on page 61 to guide your scheduling options.

Back: Warm up with wide-grip pulldowns and then move to the seated cable rows, same set and rep guidelines as with the leg program. The goal is to hit the muscle just hard enough to make some gains and then advance to the next muscle group. Keep your form strict. Go for a full contraction and a complete stretch. On Day 2, you'll do one-arm dumbbell rows and close-grip pullups or wide-grip pulldowns. You can substitute T-bar rows for dumbbell rows if you're feeling adventurous. Never get locked into doing the same program over and over again. Remember that boredom is one of the main reasons why women binge on exercise instead of treating it as an organic part of a healthy lifestyle.

Chest: Warm up with the barbell bench press and then hop over to the incline bench for some incline flyes—same movement as dumbbell flyes, only this time you're on an incline bench to shape your upper chest. Keep the weight fairly light, as you're moving through the workout quickly and efficiently.

One of the things I have noticed in training people in the gym is that most everyone grabs for the heavy weights right off the bat. What's the point? You're defeating the purpose of the 30-minute workout. Light weights and strict form will build tone and endurance—an excellent combination. You need time to build mass—don't try to plow through a heavy weight session when you're under the gun.

On chest Day 2 you'll do the pec deck as the warm-up and the incline barbell bench press to pack on some mass. Feel free to change the exercises around—pick and choose from the chest movements elsewhere in the body-sculpting plan to tailor the perfect 30-minute workout to suit your goals and objectives.

Shoulders, Biceps, Triceps, Abs and Calves: For the smaller body parts you'll drop down to only one exercise. That's all you really need. For shoulders, alternate seated military presses (Day 1) and front or lateral raises (Day 2); for biceps, go back and forth between barbell curls (Day 1) and barbell preacher curls (Day 2); for triceps, vary your triceps pressdowns (Day 1) with kickbacks or bench dips (Day 2). With abs, you should go from an upper-ab specialty like cable crunches (Day 1) into a lower-ab exercise like lying leg raises (Day 2). Finish with either standing or seated calf raises (Day 1) and donkey calf raises (Day 2).

This is a program that's especially geared to a woman's needs. A 30-minute workout for a man would focus primarily on heavy free-weight lifts that would pack on the beef. That's the last thing most women are looking for in a conditioning program. Our goal is to shape and tone the muscle, sculpting it for a strong and feminine look.

THE 30-MINUTE WORKOUT IN REVIEW

Warm-up: 10 minutes on treadmill, stationary bike or stairclimber at about 65 percent of your max heart rate (*220 minus your age equals your max heart rate*).

Beginners: Do 1 set of each exercise.

Intermediates: Do 2 to 3 sets of each exercise.

Advanced: Do 4 sets of each exercise.

Cool-down: Stretch for 5 to 10 minutes.

Day 1

Exercise	Sets	Reps
Leg extension (shaping) (see p. 26)	1–4	8–12
Leg press or squat (building) (see p. 30)	1–4	8–12
Wide-grip pulldown (back building)	1–4	8–12
Seated cable row (back shaping)	1–4	8–12
Barbell bench press* (chest building)	1–4	8–12
Incline flye* (chest shaping) (description on p. 60)	1–4	8–12
Seated military press (shoulders)	1–4	8–12
Barbell curls (biceps) Triceps pressdown (see p. 19)	1–4	8–12
Cable crunch (abs)	1–4	15–25
Seated or standing calf raise (see pps. 40–43)	1–4	15–25

Superset exercises: Do one set of bench presses, take 3 to 5 seconds of rest, then do one set of flyes. Repeat this back-and-forth format for 3 sets.

Day 2

Exercise*	Sets	Reps
Lunge (leg shaping) (see p. 35)	1–4	8–12 per leg
Leg curl Hamtractor (hamstring building)	1–4	8–12
One-arm dumbbell row (see p. 123)	1–4	8–12
Close-grip pull-up (see p. 123) or Wide-grip pulldown	1–4	8–12
Pec deck (chest shaping)	1–4	8–12
Incline barbell bench press (chest building)	1–4	8–12
Front or seated lateral raise (shoulders)	1–4	8–12
Barbell preacher curls (biceps) (see p. 125)	1–4	8–12
Triceps kickback or bench dip	1–4	8–12
Lying leg raise (abs) (see p. 47)	1–4	15–25
Donkey calf raise (see p. 38)	1–14	15–25

•Feel free to superset exercises or substitute other choices from the body-sculpting program.

Schedule: Do this 30-minute plan four days per week for one month as a break from your regular program, or as a get-in-and-out-of-the-gym-total-body-pumper on those days when you don't have enough time to do your regular workout. For example, on Monday and Friday, do the Day 1 program, and on Wednesday and Sunday, do the Day 2 program.

The 30-Minute (Beginner) Workout—Day 1

A

B

WIDE-GRIP PULLDOWN

Emphasis: *lats (latissimus dorsi)* Sit at a pulldown station with a wide-grip bar attached (*photo A*). Pull the bar down behind your head to your upper back (*photo B*), hold for the contraction, then slowly return to the full-stretch position and repeat.

A

SEATED CABLE ROW
Emphasis: *lats and middle back* Sit on the floor in front of a low cable pulley. Grasp the handles with a close grip—hands spaced just an inch or two apart—while holding the close-grip handles that are attached to the low pulley, and place your feet against the foot pads for support, knees slightly bent (*photo A*). Now pull the handle back to your upper abdomen (*photo B*). Slowly return to the starting position and repeat.

B

A

B

BARBELL BENCH PRESS

Emphasis: *overall chest* Lie on a bench with a barbell at arm's length over your chest (*photo A*). Slowly lower the bar to your upper chest (*photo B*). Once the bar touches your chest, slowly press the bar back up to the starting position. Inhale as you lower the bar; exhale on the way back up.

A

B

CABLE CRUNCH

Emphasis: *upper abdominals* Get down on your knees in front a cable pulley with a rope handle attached. Begin with the rope at forehead level (*photo A*) and crunch your abs as you lift the weight—the handle will end up at chin level (*photo B*). Exhale at the bottom, return to the starting position and repeat.

The 30-Minute (Beginner) Workout—Day 2

A

B

SEATED LATERAL RAISE
Emphasis: *side (medial) deltoid* Sit on a flat bench with a dumbbell in each hand (*photo A*). Lift the weights out to the sides (*photo B*), up to shoulder height. Slowly lower your arms to the starting position and repeat.

A

SEATED MILITARY PRESS

Emphasis: *front deltoids* Sit on a flat bench with a dumbbell in each hand, palms facing forward (*photo A*). Press the dumbbells up directly over your head, leaving a slight bend in your elbows (*photo B*). Return to the starting position and repeat. *Variation:* See Standing Military Press in Chapter 4, Portable Workouts.

B

A

LEG CURL/HAMTRACTOR

Emphasis: *hamstrings* The hamtractor (*illustrated*) is a new version of the old lying leg curl. With the hamtractor, you place your feet above the pads (legs out straight) while holding the crossbar of the machine for support (*photo A*). Then you kick your legs back (*photo B*) to contract your hamstrings. Exhale as you contract; inhale as you release the weight. In a *standard leg curl* (not shown), you lie face-down on a leg-curl machine. Curl the weight toward your buttocks, slowly lower the weight and repeat. Either exercise will do a good job of working your hamstrings.

B

A

B

PEC DECK

Emphasis: *chest* Sit at a pec-deck machine with your arms holding the handles, your elbows slightly bent, your upper arms parallel to the floor (*photo A*). Bring the handles toward each other, squeezing your chest muscles for a full contraction (*photo B*). Return to the starting position and repeat.

INCLINE BARBELL BENCH PRESS
Emphasis:
upper chest

Lie back on an incline bench. Lift the bar off the rack and lower it to your collarbone or upper chest (*photo A*). Press the weight up to arm's length over your upper chest (*photo B*), then return to the starting position and repeat.

A

B

FRONT RAISE

Emphasis: *front deltoids* Hold a dumbbell in each hand, arms hanging down at your sides, palms facing your thighs. Lift one dumbbell up to just above shoulder level (*photo*), pause for the contraction, then repeat on the other arm, switching back and forth until you've completed your set.

CHAPTER 4

Portable Workouts for Women on the Move

The whole point of this chapter is to prove to people that they can get an effective workout at home. All it takes is a little creativity and motivation to train at home, without going to a health club. All those high-tech machines at the gym are an invaluable resource, but there's something to be said for the simplicity and portability of dumbbells.

Most of the fan mail I get includes a few pointed questions:

- "How can I get an effective workout at home?"
- "While on vacation, is it possible to train in a hotel room with a minimum amount of equipment?"

- "Is working out on the beach as fun and effective as it looks?"

All of the questions are easily answered with an emphatic "Yes!" Women have many reasons for not wanting to go to the gym—a lack of time or motivation, the responsibility of caring for the kids and a low level of self-confidence are the three I hear the most. I know all about the reasons for not going to the gym. I've used them all. No matter. All you need is a pair of dumbbells and full-body workout is right at your fingertips.

You can train in a hotel room, your living room, at the beach (as you will see in the photos in this chapter), or in your backyard if the weather is nice.

The trick to training only with dumbbells and still making gains is to increase the number of repetitions you perform of each exercise. Now if you're lifting at home, yes, you can use adjustable dumbbells that will enable you to increase the weight on exercises like bench presses and one-arm rows.

But let's say you're going on vacation and you want to bring your dumbbells along for the trip. Can you imagine lugging those 30-pound monsters through the lobby of your hotel? Me neither. The solution is to stick with the easy-to-carry 10-pound weights and to lift in the high-rep range. You'll feel a good pump and enjoy the benefits of a regular weight workout—without expending the time and energy it requires to head to the gym.

Circuit training is the other on-the-road training tactic to use—do one set of bench presses for 20 reps, for example, then move right on to your flyes for 20 reps, then do your front raises for 20 reps, and keep flowing through the exercises until you've completed them all. Take a short break, stretch your muscles a little and repeat the circuit.

This circuit training mode offers several perks: It takes less time to blow through the entire workout; you burn calories while you add muscle mass, as you're training faster and more efficiently; and you'll stay more focused on your objective—completing the workout and moving on with the rest of your busy day.

If you don't have dumbbells with you on the road, there's no reason to mail in the idea of working up a sweat. Push-ups, crunches, chair dips, pull-ups, running and doing lunges and squats without weight are all good training options, especially if you're stuck in a hotel room.

You'd be surprised at how much you can do in the room to get a good workout. Grab that chair at the desk and get going with 3 to 4 sets of *chair dips* for your triceps. It's exactly the same exercise as the flat-bench dips you do in the gym. Being a little resourceful and imaginative will get you in shape anywhere, anytime.

Just stand with your back to the seat of the chair, place your hands behind you on the chair, and ease down, bending your knees, until your butt is resting against the edge, just below the level of your hands. Then press back up to the starting position, contracting your triceps.

Now get down on the floor and do some push-ups. Pump out one set with your hands shoulder-width apart. This works your chest. Then make a triangle with your hands (thumbs and index fingers lightly touching each other), bring your elbows close to your sides, and pump out a set of *close-grip push-ups* for triceps. Alternate the two variations with regular push-ups (see p. 91) for a total of 4 to 5 sets, as many reps as you can handle. Advanced body sculptors should try doing push-ups with their feet up on a chair for added resistance.

As to lower-body training without weights, the lunge and squat are a piece of cake. Here's how to do the hotel-room lunge: Spread your feet shoulder-width apart, your toes pointing directly in front of you. Slide your left foot forward, about two shoulder-widths in front of your right. With your back (right) leg remaining slightly bent, heel raised, bend your left knee until the left thigh is parallel to the ground. At this point, your left thigh and shin should be at a 90-degree angle. Straighten your left leg about halfway up and then return to parallel. Do as many of these as you can, then switch sides.

The *hotel-room squat* is much the same as the one you do in the gym. Just follow correct form, bending your knees over—not beyond—your toes until your thighs are parallel to the ground.

Then ease back up to the top and repeat for 20 reps or so for 4 to 5 sets.

You'd be surprised at how easy it is to work your body without even stopping to think about it. I do calf raises—go up on my tippy-toes and then come back down—while I'm brushing my teeth. I always walk the stairs instead of taking the elevator. I'll walk a mile or two to go to the store instead of driving. It's the little things that make a big difference.

SETTING UP A HOME GYM

One of the most frequently asked questions I hear from women who watch the show is: "What do I need to set up a home gym?" Not much, really. A few essential items:

- A basic bench that can be set at an incline angle for bench presses and flyes. Even a piano bench can work temporarily.
- A barbell with some 10, 20 and 30-pound weight plates (optional).
- Two sets of dumbbells, one light for travel and one heavy for more serious home workouts. Or you can buy dumbbells that

are adjustable to accommodate a variety of poundages.

- A weight belt to support your abdominal muscles and lower back when doing squats and bench presses. A pair of gloves to improve your grip is another plus.
- A mirror that will allow you to check your form while you lift.
- Running or walking shoes. Take a walk around town instead of sitting on the couch and collapsing after a hard day. Stroll over to your local high school and run or walk up the bleachers. There's so much you can do without going to the health club and investing all that money in a membership.
- Stationary bikes, treadmills and stairclimbers come in all sizes, levels of sophistication and price ranges. Buy one that you'll actually use at least four times a week, 20 minutes per day.

I think of the indoor cardio equipment as more of a bad-weather option. My advice is to do your cardiovascular exercise outdoors; the fresh air and sunshine is a fantastic motivator. There have been many studies that prove that people who are exposed to sunshine are happier and have more energy.

KIANA'S PORTABLE BODY-SCULPTING COMPANION

The On-the-Road Circuit Training System

Do 1 set of 20 repetitions per movement, then immediately advance to the next exercise. Take a minimal rest—about 60 seconds—between circuits. Repeat the circuit three times. Or you can split up the exercises and do 3 to 4 sets of 20 reps for each, as time allows.

Dumbbell squat
Lunge (see p. 35)
Dumbbell bench press
Dumbbell flye
Wide-grip push-up
Two-arm dumbbell row
Dumbbell pullover
Front raise
Standing military press
Dumbbell curl
Triceps kickback (see p. 15)
Two-arm dumbbell extension (see p. 17)
Portable crunch
V-up (see pp. 49–50)
Lying leg raise (see p. 47)

Kiana's Hotel-Room Workout (Can Be Done Without Weights)

Exercise	Sets	Reps
Bench or chair dip (see p. 98)	3–5	15–25
Wide-grip push-up	2–3	Max
Close-grip push-up (see p. 123)	2–3	Max
Lunge	4–5	15–25
Squat	4–5	15–25

Portable
Workout

DUMBBELL CURL

Emphasis: *biceps* Grasp the dumbbells with a palms-in grip, letting them rest at your sides. Curl the dumbbell in your left arm up to shoulder level (*as in photo*), return to the starting position and then immediately raise the other dumbbell to the level of your right shoulder. Do an equal number of reps on each arm.

WIDE-GRIP PUSH-UP

Emphasis: *chest* Place your palms on the ground, fingers forward, directly underneath and slightly farther apart than your shoulders. Push your body weight off the ground by straightening your elbows.

A

B

DUMBBELL FLYE
Emphasis: *chest* Holding the dumbbells overhead and facing each other (*photo A*), gradually lower the weights out to the side in a semicircular motion (*photo B*). Retrace the arc to the starting position and repeat.

A

B

DUMBBELL PULLOVER

Emphasis: *chest*   Hold a dumbbell with both hands at arm's length over your chest (*photo A*). From this position, slowly extend the weight back over your head and lower it until it touches the ground behind you (*photo B*). Return to the starting position and repeat.

TWO-ARM DUMBBELL ROW *(also known as an Upright Row)*

Emphasis: *trapezius and front deltoids* Hold two dumbbells in front of you about six inches apart, with your palms facing your body. Bending your elbows (*as in the photo*), pull the dumbbells up to chest level, then lower slowly. Repeat.

PORTABLE CRUNCH
Emphasis: *upper abdominals* Lie on a flat surface, cross your arms over your chest, bend your knees and crunch forward, bringing your rib cage toward your pelvis (*as in the photo*). Return to the starting position and repeat.

PORTABLE SIDE CRUNCH
Emphasis: *obliques, serratus* Lie on a flat surface, cross your left leg over your right knee and bring your right elbow toward your left knee (*as in the photo*). Switch sides and repeat.

STANDING MILITARY PRESS
Emphasis: *front deltoids* Grasp two dumbbells and turn your palms to face each other. Lift the dumbbells over your head, and lower. Repeat.

DUMBBELL SQUAT
Emphasis: *quadriceps, gluteals, lower back*

You can do this on the beach. Hold two dumbbells, without bending your arms, and squat until your thighs are parallel to the sand. Then return to the starting position and repeat. Lower and raise yourself slowly and smoothly; don't lurch down and up.

FRONT RAISE
Emphasis: *shoulders, front deltoids* Grasp the dumbbell palm down, and raise it in front of you to shoulder level. Repeat.

BENCH OR CHAIR DIP
Emphasis: *triceps*

Do this in your hotel room! Place your feet on the floor, with knees bent; your hands rest on a flat bench or two chairs behind you for support (*photo A*). Lower your body until you feel a contraction in your triceps (*photo B*); repeat.

A

B

A

B

DUMBBELL BENCH PRESS

Emphasis: *chest* Lie on a flat surface (in a gym you'd do this on a flat bench; when you're on vacation, though, a floor or the warm sand is fine) with a dumbbell in each hand. Hold the dumbbells at arm's length, palms facing forward (*photo A*). Lower the dumbbells to the sides of your chest (*photo B*), push back up to the starting position and repeat.

CHAPTER 5

Cross Training with Kiana

Cross training, or blending different sports into a comprehensive exercise routine, is a great way to add freshness to your workouts. It forces you to hit your muscles at a different angle and with a different mode of resistance. And, even more important, it adds a whole lot of fun and competition to your every-day weight-training ritual.

Consistency is the key to cross training. You can't be a slave to the weights or the exercise bike. Mix things up. Shake up the standard program. Try a new sport. You'll stay motivated and enjoy your strength-building routines more if you diversify your menu of activities. And by being consistent in whatever you do, you'll make staying fit and healthy your lifestyle.

That's the whole point of this book—to make you consistent and dedicated to exercising regularly and eating healthily. Make exercising and eating right a priority. It is a lifestyle approach to health and fitness. Try new sports and exercises to stay one step ahead of boredom and burnout. I never lose my focus because I'm always into trying something new, different and exciting.

Tennis, skiing, cycling, in-line skating and boxercise—the sports covered in this chapter—give you the chance to get outdoors and/or work out with other people. Being competitive is a good motivator, whether you're on the tennis court or on the ski slopes.

My parents are great at all sports; they taught me to enjoy physical exercise and to treat it as a pleasure, not as a chore that has to be merely tolerated.

I want you to feel the same way about sports and exercise. Take what you learn in the weight room and transfer it directly to improving your sports performance. This is what Martina Navratilova has done at tennis; she trains with weights and as a runner to improve her strength and cardiovascular endurance. Women athletes have amazing physical potential. Don't be afraid to use weights to take your game up to the next level of success.

Cross training also comes in handy when you're traveling. Your hotel doesn't have a weight room? No problem. Just put on a good pair of running shoes, get up a little early and go for a jog. Or, if there's a tennis court at the hotel, that gives you another option. Options—the more things you can tap into to get a good workout, the better your chances of escaping the inside of your hotel room.

Cross training forces you to be versatile and flexible. You're improving your heart rate, you're blending aerobic (endurance) and anaerobic (strength) exercise into a unified program; you're relying on strength training to build muscle; and you're using your favorite sports to improve flexibility, quickness and speed.

KIANA ON TENNIS

This is my favorite sport—as you may have already guessed by now. I started playing at seven and haven't stopped since. Tennis requires agility and both upper- and lower-body strength. And it also requires a high level of cardiovascular conditioning.

I run like crazy when I'm on the court—back and forth and from side to side. So my plan of action for tennis players is to run three or four times a week to build endurance. And I'll also do speed drills—sprinting from one side of the court to the other and from the service line to the base line of the court. Just short, quick bursts of speed and sudden acceleration. Always keep moving on your toes to improve your footwork.

Cardio conditioning is much more important than the strength training for tennis. Run for 40 minutes, three or four times per week.

Your strength goal is to lift with high reps for endurance. Do some light arm work to increase your biceps/triceps/shoulder strength and coordination. Run in the soft sand—if you're near a beach—to increase your calf strength and endurance. Your calves—believe it or not—take the brunt of all that lateral pounding when you go back and forth to return the side-to-side volleys.

Speed drills: Put one tennis ball on the base line (the line at the back of the court), one at the service line (the line at the back of the box to which you aim your serve) and one on each of the doubles lines on either side of the court. Now get down on your toes in a squatting position—the ready position for how you'd return a shot—and run from one ball to another, keeping low, touching the ball and moving laterally, backwards and forwards. Repeat for five minutes. Take a breather. Repeat several times. This improves your lateral movement, while also enhancing agility.

Strength training emphasis: Biceps barbell curls, lying triceps extensions, triceps kickbacks, lateral raises (optional), military presses (optional), bench presses (optional), leg presses (optional), squats, leg curls, wide-grip pulldowns, hyperextensions (for lower back) and seated calf raises. Lift for 3 sets of 15 reps. Keep the weight light; heavy weights will throw your coordination out of whack. It's much like a jump shooter on a basketball team who lifts really heavy weights and then tries to nail those long three-point shots. Forget it. Tennis is a finesse game, not a muscle game.

Andre Agassi, Jim Courier, Boris Becker, Michael Chang, Martina Navratilova and Gabriela Sabatini all have powerfully built legs, but their upper bodies are lean and well-proportioned, not overly muscle-bound. You should aspire to the same aesthetic and functional objective, if playing superb tennis is what you're after. You certainly don't need huge arms to serve well and with speed and accuracy.

Cross Training for Tennis

Objective: Use this low-volume weight training program to build adequate upper- and lower-body strength and endurance. Keep reps high to avoid packing on too much muscle mass. Lift two to four times per week, but not on days you're going to play a lot of tennis.

Supplement the weight work with running—40 minutes per day, three or four times per week, stair climbing and the aforementioned speed drills.

Exercise	Sets	Reps
Squat	3	15
Seated calf raise	5	15
Biceps barbell curl	3	15
Lying triceps extension	3	15
Triceps kickback	3	15
Leg curl	3	15
Wide-grip pulldown	3	15
Hyperextension or deadlift	3	15

KIANA ON SKIING

Skiing requires considerable lower-body and back strength. I learned this the hard way while skiing slalom races on the UCLA ski team. Cutting those razor-sharp turns to squeak through the slalom gates puts a tremendous stress on the quadriceps, calves and hamstrings.

The best line of defense against an injury is to train on the track and in the weight room to get ready for the painful pleasures of the ski slopes. Injury prevention and strength training are key.

Squats really help a lot. The stronger your quads, the harder you can carve a turn and the faster you can ski down a hill. The quadriceps muscles help you get control over your skis, a big plus when you're racing downhill over moguls and ice, or even on the soft, fast powder.

The only time I ever made great strides as a competitive skier, in fact, was when I started squatting heavy. I would switch up my weight training with low reps and heavy weight one week, high reps and low weight the next. Strength (from heavy weights) and endurance (from light weights) are both essential to safe and efficient skiing.

And remember that you're going to ski at a high altitude. Hill running is one way to improve your cardio endurance. Try running up a hill five times and walking down five times. Then try some interval running with 440s, 220s and 100s on a track. Or you can run a measured distance by counting telephone poles; vary your speed as you complete one interval and begin on the next.

In general, leg training is your number-one priority as a skier. Lunges, squats, leg extensions and leg curls are all great. Do biceps curls and triceps extensions for your arms. If you have a weak area—most women need help with their glutes and thighs—then you'll want to lift with a heavier weight for that targeted problem spot (see Chapter 2).

For your cardio conditioning, do 20 minutes of running, three to four times per week.

Cross training options: In-line skating, ice skating, cycling. I like to run in the soft sand. The ski training machine is another excellent training option. Always stretch your lower back and thighs before you ski or run.

Cross Training for Skiing

Objective: Put the emphasis on perfecting your squatting technique and building your lower-body and back strength and stamina. Follow the recommended weight-training program and supplement with an eclectic cardio routine—running in the sand or on the track, sprinting, running up hills, doing interval training and running up bleachers or training indoors on the stairclimber or ski trainer.

Do both cardio and weights three to five times per week. Cut back on the weight during ski season.

Exercise	Sets	Reps
Squat	3	15
Lunge	3	15
Leg extension	3	15
Leg curl	3	15
Deadlift	3	15
Hyperextension	3	15
Biceps curl	3	15
Triceps curl	3	15

KIANA ON CYCLING

I was on the cycling team at UC Santa Barbara—that's where I spent my first two years in college before transferring to UCLA. I was a distance cyclist, and this was before mountain bikes came into fashion.

Leg training is the main event for cyclists of all persuasions. Focus on long-distance running, four or five times per week. That's what I do. And I'm no speed demon on the cross-country trails—an 8-minute-mile pace is about all I can handle. That's almost comparable to fast walking, which is a perfectly adequate alternative to running if your joints can't handle the pounding.

Another good cardio and lower-body training option is the stationary bike, the perfect cross training complement to outdoor cycling. Keep your RPMs (pedal revolutions per minute) high and vary your speed and level of difficulty. Most new stationary bikes can be easily programmed to simulate any cycling situation, from the most gentle slope to the most challenging hill. Flip-flop back and forth from easy to hard and from slow to fast. Challenge yourself to improve with each workout. Always shoot for at least 20 minutes each time you hop on the bike.

As for strength training, the emphasis is on building strength and stamina in your lower back, legs and arms—you're leaning forward in that hunched-over position so you'd better be comfortable with all those vibrations, especially if you're into mountain biking.

Calf raises—donkeys, seated and standing—leg extensions, squats and leg presses are what you need for your lower body. Seated cable rows improve your upper-back strength while hyperextensions and/or deadlifts add stability to the lower spine. Triceps extensions and biceps curls give your arms the strength you need to steer and brake with authority. And wrist curls with a barbell and reverse curls help to improve the resiliency of your forearms as they cope with the vibrations caused by uneven terrain.

Stretch after you cycle to loosen up your quads, calves, back and hamstrings; the last thing you need is to wake up in the middle of the night with a terrible muscle cramp. Ouch!

Cross Training for Cycling

Objective: Lift weights at least two days per week with the following program to improve overall strength and power. Run or power walk four days per week for at least 20 minutes per day. Cross train on the stationary bike and play around with interval training, varying speed and resistance to simulate actual riding conditions.

A word to mountain bikers: You need to do more for your upper body than your touring counterparts. The forces of gravity are working against you as you climb those steep hills, and going up on the pedals puts a considerable strain on your lower back, shoulders and forearms.

Exercise	Sets	Reps
Leg extension	3	15
Leg curl	3	15
Calf raise		
Standing	1	15
Seated	1	15
Donkey	1	15
Hyperextension or deadlift	3	15
Seated cable row	3	15
Mountain bikers:		
Reverse curls	3	15
Wrist curls	3	15
Triceps extensions	3	15
Biceps barbell curls	3	15

KIANA ON IN-LINE SKATING

This is the fastest-growing sport in the United States. It's very big in Hawaii! I love to in-line skate, or blade, because you do it outdoors, it's easy, fun and an incredible workout for the legs and calves. It requires balance and coordination. And it's a wonderful cross training tool for skiers and tennis players—the balance it teaches will help you maintain a firm center of gravity over your skis; the push-off motion is ideal for the acceleration you need to lunge after tennis balls. Overall, in-line skating is one of the most intriguing new sports to catch on in the past twenty years—and it's much more accessible than mountain biking.

Don't put on in-line skates until you're in reasonably good shape. I recommend light squats, leg presses, leg extensions, leg curls and lunges. Stretch your quadriceps, hamstrings and calves before you blade. And follow the standard safety measures that go with the rules of the game—wear all the necessary protective gear and don't blade in heavy traffic or in places where bikes can run you over. I wear wrist guards, knee pads and elbow pads as an insurance policy against bruises and other nagging injuries. Why take chances?

Cardiovascular conditioning for in-line skaters: Nothing too radical, as blading is a good cardio workout in itself. I like to run two or three times per week for 20 minutes to work up a sweat and get the heart rate up into its target zone.

You can try this *skating drill* to improve your turning skill and to condition lateral quickness: grab a pair of traffic cones or two juice cans and place them about 10 feet apart. Start with two to three quick-step crossovers to each cone, making sure your weight rest on your toes. Then reverse. Do 5 reps of 10 seconds each, followed by a 5-second rest.

Cross Training for In-Line Skating

Objective: Improve your lower-body strength with two or three days per week of weight training. Reps stay high to enhance endurance, rather than building any new muscle mass. Stick with two or three days of cardio, 20 minutes per day, and work on your blading skills with the specialized drill I recommended earlier.

Exercise	Sets	Reps
Squat	3	15
Lunge	3	15
Leg extension	3	15
Leg curl	3	15
Leg press	3	15

KIANA ON BOXERCISE

Okay, I know what you're thinking: What the heck is boxercise? It's nothing more than using a heavy bag and a speed bag to train upper body strength and agility. Many health clubs now offer boxing aerobics, which blends low-impact aerobics with punching drills. No gloves or equipment is used in these classes. I prefer to go to a boxing gym, work with a trainer and just run through a few simple punching combinations.

I got into boxercise two years ago when I was auditioning for a national TV commercial. I also dabbled in kickboxing, a hybrid of several martial arts styles with a lot of high kicking. Now I just do it for fun—and it's an effective way to relieve stress after a hard day at the office or on the set of a TV show.

Boxing techniques demand chest and shoulder strength, powerful arms and quick feet. You'll work with heavier weights than in the other cross training programs and focus on upper-body lifts. But you don't want to get too muscle-bound—the goal is to be lean and strong. Repetitions stay in the 10 to 12 range, a nice middle ground for blending strength with endurance.

For your cardio conditioning, skip rope, climb stairs, cycle or run at least four times per week. Shoot for 20 to 40 minutes per workout.

Boxing Drills

Here are a few basic boxing techniques that you can try at home. If I can do it, you can do it too!

The left jab: Drive off the ball of your right foot as you step forward with your left. Rotate your left shoulder while executing the punch with that arm. Always punch in a straight line, making sure your arm is extended at impact. Punch through your imaginary opponent and don't drop your right hand. After completing the follow-through, return your left hand to its initial position and repeat.

The left hook: From a classic boxing stance, dip your right knee slightly and square your hips toward your imaginary opponent. Transfer your weight to the ball of your left (front) foot, while you pivot right and launch the punch. Rotate your hips and shoulders from square to sideways toward your opponent while you continue to pivot. Keep your left (hooking) elbow bent at a 90-degree angle and your head down on the follow-through. Your chin is guarded by your right fist and left shoulder.

The straight right: Drive off the ball of your right foot as you step forward with your left. With your left side working like a hinge, rotate your right hip and shoulder toward your imaginary opponent as you fully extend your right arm. Be sure your chin is tucked. Avoid lowering your left arm as you punch with your right. After the punch, quickly return your right arm to its "ready" position.

Cross Training for Boxercise

Objective: Increase your lean body mass with a moderate upper-body weight training program, two times per week (on days you don't do your boxercise). Improve your cardio endurance with a mixed program of running, climbing stairs, jumping rope and cycling.

Exercise	Sets	Reps
Triceps kickback	3	10
Triceps pressdown	3	10
Lying triceps extension	3	10
Biceps barbell curl	3	10
Barbell preacher curl	3	10
Seated military press	3	10
Lateral raise	3	10
Front raise	3	10
Barbell bench press	3	10

Take classes at your local health club to reinforce this program. Trust me; this is a great way to get in shape, while burning calories and relieving stress.

KIANA'S CROSS TRAINING CALORIE COUNTER

How many calories do you burn per hour in your favorite sport? The exact number is relative to your age, caloric intake, fitness level and metabolic rate. But here's an easy-to-follow guideline (calories are approximations) that will give you some idea of how effectively your sport is helping you lose weight and evolve into body-sculpting shape.

Aerobic Fitness

Activities	Calories Burned per Hour
Hiking	247
Mountain biking	385
Road-bike touring	385
Tennis	357
Running (10-minute-mile pace)	561
Swimming	330
Basketball (half court)	336
Aerobics class	495
Volleyball	384
Power walking	478
Racquetball	495
Stair climbing	330
Jumping rope	495
Hill climbing	396

Flexibility

Activities	Calories Burned per Hour
Dancing (funk)	495
Yoga	100
Judo/karate	360

Strength

Activities	Calories Burned per Hour
Rock climbing	485
Board sailing	470
Kayaking	317
Swimming (interval training)	330
Waterskiing	552
Weight training	330
Calisthenics	342
Rowing	302

Sport/Skill

Activities	Calories Burned per Hour
White-water rafting	310
Roller skating	384
Volleyball	384
Skydiving	290
Golf (walking the course)	366
Horseback riding	186
Snorkeling	220
Archery	200
Sailing	210
Bowling	222
Canoeing (4 mph)	504

CHAPTER 6

Advanced Body Sculpting in Action

Now it's time to put the entire system into perspective. I've been working diligently for years to improve my appearance and to take fitness to a higher level. For me, it's more than just doing robotic sets and reps of countless exercises. I hope it's evident that I really enjoy what I do. I can't fake that enthusiasm. The smile on my face is pure and genuine.

Women always come up to me and ask for the secret to my success—is it hard work, genetics, luck of the draw? Thanks to my parents, I'm blessed with pretty good genetics; my parents are healthy, active and energetic. But the bottom line for me is hard work and dedication. I'd be just a skinny girl with a nice personality if it wasn't for my years of going to the gym and lifting with weights—scientifically and methodically—in pursuit of my personal best.

I want to share my personal program with you; it's the culmination of the past ten years of experimentation and trial and error. When you see me in magazines or on television, it all looks so easy and effortless, but I have my own moments of doubt and concern. The only way to break through those barriers is to keep striving for success.

KIANA'S ADVANCED WORKOUT

I'll lift three days in succession, take a day off, and then lift three days in a row again; each body part gets my attention twice per week.

I devised this three days on, one day off strategy after consulting with exercise physiologists and a host of bodybuilders at Gold's Gym in Venice. But I didn't just blindly go along with what these experts told me. I'd give everything a try and then fine-tune the program to suit my specific goals.

I settled on three exercises per body part: two mass builders and one sculpting movement. The sculpting exercise makes the program more accessible to a woman's need to remain feminine no matter how much weight she lifts.

Day 1: Chest/Shoulders/Triceps/Abs
Day 2: Legs/Calves—this gives your upper body a break
Day 3: Back/Biceps/Abs
Day 4: Take a break from lifting, but try to bike, run or do some other type of cardio-conditioning recreational activity.

I hit calves and abs every other workout. These body parts can bounce back a lot quicker than the others—and they need the consistent and frequent resistance if you hope to make any inroads in the body-sculpting adventure.

If you're ready to take a whack at this advanced program, let me give you a piece of advice: Forget about socializing in the gym—there's too much work to do.

I like to wear headphones and listen to my favorite motivational music. Focus! Block out everything that interferes with your link between the mind and the muscle you're training. This is your time to get the most out of your workout.

Priority Training

Every woman knows her strengths and weaknesses. I love to train my shoulders, but triceps are quite another story. So on chest/triceps/shoulder day, I'll hit my triceps right after my chest

while I'm still strong and fresh. I can go at my shoulders at the end because I know that I'll still be able to handle the workload. I want you to do this same thing with your training program. Assess what needs the attention and devote your time and energy to that particular area. Train the most difficult areas first.

I'm asking you to lift six days a week in this advanced program—that's a big time commitment. But perhaps your shoulders are toned enough to miss a workout, yet your triceps are lagging far behind the rest of your physique. Prioritize. Everyone is going to miss a workout every now and then. I know it's not the end of the world if I can't find time for every single exercise. All I'm asking is that you give it your best, that you dedicate yourself to being as consistent as you can with this routine.

Shake It Up

As with the other workouts we've discussed, it's essential to switch the exercises and poundages on a regular basis. I'll lift heavy with low repetitions one week, light with high repetitions the next week.

The idea is to keep your body guessing about what's coming next and to derive the strength benefits of heavy weights and the endurance benefits of light weights. The best of both worlds—why not enjoy the pleasures of a sexy, shapely body and the strength and self-confidence that comes with an aggressive cross training program?

Listen to Your Body

Don't deny your body the impulse to tell you how it's feeling on any given day in the gym. You can't be dogmatic about your physical condition-ing. The training process must reflect how you respond to stimulation at a particular moment. If the bar feels too heavy at 45—even if you ordinarily bench press that weight with ease—drop down in weight and increase the reps.

Feeling burned out after just two sets of bench press? Streamline the workout with 3 sets of good dips and 20 minutes on the bike, and then head home knowing you made the best of the situation. Next time will be better. Show yourself some forgiveness and understanding; trust your instincts and believe in your ability to overcome obstacles.

Nothing comes easy in life. Stick with this program for as long as it takes to reach your goals. Give it your all. I want to be there for you on those days when you're ready to quit. I'll always be your personal trainer—as long as you stay consistent with my ideals and remain true to yourself.

THE ADVANCED BODY-SCULPTING WORKOUT

Do 12 to 15 sets for the large muscle groups: chest, back and legs. For exercises like the bench press and squat, where you know you're going to lift heavier, always do a light warm-up set of 20 reps with little or no weight on the bar.

Do 6 to 8 sets for the other body parts.

Alternate light weeks (12 to 15 reps per exercise, using lighter weights) with heavy weeks (6 to 8 reps with heavier weights).

Note: the following chart represents a heavy week of training.

Warm-up: 10 minutes on the treadmill, light and easy—about 65 percent of your heart-rate maximum (*220 minus your age equals your max heart rate*).

Day 1: Chest/Triceps/Shoulders (Heavy)
Chest:

Exercise	Sets	Reps
Bench press	4–5	6–8
Incline barbell bench press	4–5	6–8
Pec deck	4–5	6–8

Substitutions: Dumbbell flyes, incline flyes, decline bench presses, cable crossovers and parallel bar dips.

Triceps:

Exercise	Sets	Reps
Triceps pressdown (with rope handle)	2–3	6–8
Triceps kickback	2–3	6–8
Lying triceps extension	2–3	6–8

Substitutions: Bench dips, close-grip bench presses.

Shoulders:

Exercise	Sets	Reps
Standing or seated military press	2–3	6–8
Seated upright row	2–3	6–8
Seated lateral raise	2–3	6–8

Substitutions: Front raises, reverse flyes.

Abdominals (**perform as a circuit**):

Exercise	Sets	Reps
Crunch	3	25
Side crunch (same as portable)	3	25
V-up	3	25
Lying leg raise	3	25

Day 2: Legs/Calves
Calves (**perform as a circuit**):

Exercise	Sets	Reps
Standing calf raise	3	25
Seated calf raise	3	25
Donkey calf raise	3	25

Legs:

Exercise	Sets	Reps
Leg extension	3–4	15–18
Squat	3–4	6–8
Smith-machine squat	3–4	6–8
Deadlift	3–4	6–8

Substitutions: Lunges, lunges up onto a step, leg presses, leg curls, hamtractors.

Day 3: Back/Biceps/Abs

Back:

Exercise	Sets	Reps
T-bar row	3–5	6–8
Seated cable row	3–5	6–8
Close-grip pull-up	3–5	6–8
Hyperextension	1	20–25

Substitutions: Wide-grip pulldowns, one-arm dumbbell rows, reverse flyes.

Biceps:

Exercise	Sets	Reps
Barbell curl	2–3	6–8
Barbell preacher curl	2–3	6–8

Substitutions: Dumbbell curls, concentration curls.

Abdominals:

Repeat ab workout from Day 1.

Day 4: Focus on cardio for 45 minutes to an hour.

Day 5: Repeat Day 1.

Day 6: Repeat Day 2.

Day 7: Repeat Day 3.

Day 8: Break.

Advanced
Body Sculpting

CABLE CROSSOVER

Emphasis: *lower/middle chest* Stand between two overhead cable pulleys and grasp one handle in each hand. Lean forward slightly and extend your arms outward. Now bring your arms together—crossing one over the other (*as in the photo*)—and squeeze your chest muscles. Release, and allow your arms to slowly return to the starting position.

A

DEADLIFT

Emphasis: *hamstrings* Stand erect, with your feet just under the barbell. Then grasp the barbell with your hands just a little wider than shoulder-width, your knuckles facing the wall in front of you, and your back perfectly flat (*photo A*). Now bend your knees and slowly stand up, straightening your legs, and continue lifting the bar until your back is perfectly straight (*photo B*). Lower the weight to the floor and repeat. Inhale as you lower the weight; exhale as you stand up.

B

A

B

UPRIGHT ROW

Emphasis: *trapezius and front deltoids* Grasp a barbell with your hands about six inches apart and your palms facing your body (*photo A*). Pull the bar up to your upper chest (*photo B*). Pause, then lower the bar to the starting position and repeat. Try varying your grip (close versus wide) to work different areas of the traps and delts. *Variation*: See Two-Arm Dumbbell Row, in Chapter 4, Portable Workouts.

A

T-BAR ROW
Emphasis: *lats and trapezius (the diamond-shaped muscle covering much of your upper back)*
Bend over and grasp the handles of a T-bar—make sure your back is perfectly flat (photo A). Raise the bar to your chest (*photo B*), slowly lower and repeat.

B

CLOSE-GRIP PULL-UP

Emphasis: *lats* Assume a close grip (hands inside of shoulder-width) on the bar. Slowly lower your body until you feel a stretch in your back—your arms will begin to straighten out. Then lift your chin up above the bar (*as in photo*), arching your back slightly.

ONE-ARM DUMBBELL ROW

Emphasis: *lats and middle back*
Resting your left knee and hand on a flat bench for support, grasp a dumbbell and raise it until it reaches the outer portion of your upper abdomen, keeping your elbow close to your side (*as in photo*). Slowly lower and repeat.

A

REVERSE FLYE
Emphasis: *rear deltoid*

Grasping two dumbbells, sit on a flat
bench with your chest out over your
knees and the dumbbells together
below your thighs (*photo A*). Now bring
both dumbbells back until your arms are
straight and parallel to your shoulders
(*photo B*). Retrace the arc of the lift and
return to the starting position.

B

A

B

BARBELL PREACHER CURL

Emphasis: *biceps* Sit on a preacher curl bench and lean forward, your upper arms flat on the pad (*photo A*). Using a shoulder-width grip, curl the barbell until your biceps are fully contracted (*photos B and C in sequence*). Slowly lower and repeat.

C

A

BARBELL CURL
Emphasis: *biceps* Stand erect with a palms-up, shoulder-width grip on the barbell (*photo A*). Now slowly lift, or curl, the barbell up to shoulder height using only the biceps muscle; simply bend your elbows as you curl the bar up (*photo B*). From this fully contracted position, slowly lower the bar to the starting position.

B

A

CONCENTRATION CURL

Emphasis: *biceps* Sit on a flat bench with a dumbbell in your right hand, your right elbow resting against your right knee (*photo A*). Lift, or curl, the dumbbell up to fully contract your biceps (*photo B*). Lower and repeat with your left arm.

B

CHAPTER 7

The Body–Sculpting Diet Plan

From skinny to shapely—I've made tremendous gains in the past 10 years since my body-sculpting lifestyle began in the early 1980s. But weight training is only one part of my program; diet is, in my opinion, the underlying secret to my success.

It wasn't always easy to eat healthily. Growing up in Orange County, California, was sort of an experiment in eating junk food. My parents served me wholesome meals, but once I was out of the house it was just a question of how much junk food I could get my hands on. I was skinny. My legs were tiny. No shape; nothing but skin and bones.

My body went through some amazing changes in high school—and the changes weren't limited to my coming of age. This physical transformation leapt out of the woodwork almost overnight, it seemed, as I searched for a way to improve my tennis skills. Having played tennis since the age of seven, I went out for the tennis team. But I wanted a stronger serve, a harder groundstroke and an edge over the other girls. This was before it was "in" to lift weights to improve sports performance, but an instinctive impulse pushed me into the weight room. I just did it on a whim, really.

I started to add muscle mass pretty quickly. I developed shapely shoulders and a muscular back. People started telling me how great I looked and my adolescent ego clicked in—I wanted to get serious about my training so that I'd look even better.

You can't train all the time without craving the calories you burn during exercise. I started eating a lot of big protein meals before and after training. My weight soared from 100 to 127 pounds, though it was mostly lean body mass, not fat. I took a lot of amino acids to help build and repair muscle tissue. And before long I was competing in bodybuilding shows. I'd gained 30 pounds in just a few short years; the skinny little girl vanished in a flash.

Once I started working on television and working as a fitness model, my whole perspective on diet and training did a 180-degree turnaround. I decided to stay lean and muscular, without the extra muscle mass that detracted from my feminine shape.

My current plan is to eat smaller meals, about five or six daily, with more complex carbohydrates (especially green vegetables, fruits and whole grains) to keep my energy level constant throughout the day. I still eat my share of protein, but generally I'll wait until two hours after my workout—that's when rebuilding and repairing muscle tissue is of the utmost importance.

KIANA'S LOW-FAT HAWAIIAN COOKING

Most girls eat a bizarre diet as they're growing up. I'm no exception to that rule. But I was lucky that my family taught me the benefits of low-fat cooking. My dad is from Hawaii and my mom is Chinese; people of Asian descent tend to eat foods that are low in fat and rich in flavor: fish,

MAUI GRANOLA

I eat this for breakfast or as a snack. I can put some in a jar and carry it around with me in the car while I commute from one appointment to another. This is an easy and healthy way to snack on a busy schedule, a low-fat alternative to bingeing on fast food.

INGREDIENTS
5 cups rolled oats
1 cup wheat germ
1 cup honey
¼ cup safflower oil
½ cup raisins
½ cup pitted dates, sliced
1 cup almonds

Preheat the oven to 300 degrees. Combine and bake the oats, wheat germ, honey and safflower oil for 1 hour and 15 minutes, stirring every 15 minutes. Add the raisins, dates and almonds and bake for 15 minutes. Cool to room temperature and store in an airtight container. Makes enough for about a one-month supply. Serve with seasonal fresh fruit—papaya and guava are ideal.

lean meats and vegetables are stir-fried in just a tablespoon of oil. Low-fat, steamed white rice is the main dish, while the meat, vegetables and fish add flavor and are served in smaller portions.

The workout diet I've designed is unlike anything you've ever seen before. How many times have you heard: "Take the skin off your chicken. Eat the egg whites and throw out the yolk. Eat tuna packed in water instead of oil." Fine. But this approach gets pretty boring after a while.

Try preparing these delicious Hawaiian specialties instead of the usual low-fat fare. This is the best way I know of to stay lean and still enjoy the sensual pleasures of eating. After all, eating is one of the pleasures in life.

CHINESE CHICKEN SALAD

Perfect for a quick, low-fat lunch or dinner. I'll often prepare the chicken salad in the morning, pack it in a plastic container and bring it along to photo shoots. I never trust the random offerings of catering trucks and luncheonettes. The Chinese chicken salad is high in protein and low in salt. Almonds and tangerines add flavor and texture.

INGREDIENTS
1 can dried chow-mein noodles, or 2 ounces rice sticks and 2 tablespoons sesame oil to fry them in
1 roasted chicken, skinned, meat shredded into thin slices
4 stalks green onion, cut into ½" slivers
1 bunch cilantro, stemmed and chopped
1 large head of lettuce, shredded
3 tablespoons sesame seeds, toasted

SEASONINGS:
2 teaspoons low-sodium soy sauce
1 tablespoon sesame oil
1 teaspoon salt
3 tablespoons salad oil
½ teaspoon pepper
Juice of ½ lemon
2 teaspoons sugar (optional)

If using rice sticks instead of dried noodles: fry the sticks in oil heated to 350 degrees until they puff up—it takes no more than 1 or 2 seconds; remove and drain. Combine all the ingredients except the noodles or rice sticks in a large bowl and toss together. Add the noodles or rice sticks at the end. Serve immediately, or refrigerate packed in an airtight plastic container.

KONA BANANA EGG WHITES

An easy way to enjoy a typical Hawaiian breakfast. High in protein, low in fat and very sweet indeed. The natural fruit sugars are a delicious complement to the egg whites.

INGREDIENTS

6 eggs
1 ripe banana, mashed
1 tablespoon nonfat milk or water
½ teaspoon vanilla

Spray a nonstick skillet with nonstick cooking spray—this is a low-fat alternative to cooking with oil or butter. Heat the pan to medium-high. Separate the egg whites into a dish and fold in the mashed banana. Add the nonfat milk or water and vanilla. Stir. When the pan is hot, pour in the egg white mixture. Scramble the eggs or make an omelette. Serve with raisins or dried apples if you like.

ISLAND OATMEAL

Prepare oatmeal with apple juice instead of water; add nonfat yogurt and serve with sliced fresh papaya, guava and banana. Substitute any seasonal fruit and add nonfat milk if you like.

PINEAPPLE CHICKEN "MAUI STYLE"

A hearty lunch or dinner option. My grandmother in Maui whipped up this recipe; she's ninety-three years old and still going strong. Okay, so she doesn't lift weights. But it's safe to say her diet has kept her fit and healthy for a lifetime.

INGREDIENTS

1 pound chicken parts (preferably breasts), skinned and boned
2 tablespoons canola oil
1 stalk celery
1 large can of pineapple chunks (packed in unsweetened juice)
½ cup water
½ cup ketchup
1 tablespoon vinegar

1¼ tablespoons sugar
1 teaspoon cornstarch (for thickening)
2 teaspoons cold water (for thickening)

MARINADE:

½ teaspoon sugar
1 teaspoon low-sodium soy sauce
Dash of pepper
1 slice fresh ginger, chopped

Cut the chicken into 1½-inch cubes. Heat the oil in a wok and quickly stir-fry the chicken. Add the ingredients for the marinade, mix thoroughly and simmer for 2 minutes. Cut the celery into 1½-inch pieces; then cut each piece lengthwise into strips. Drain the pineapple, reserving the juice. Combine the pineapple juice, water, ketchup, vinegar and sugar and mix into the wok with the simmering chicken. Bring to a boil. Now add the pineapple chunks and celery slices. Cook on high heat for 1 minute. Combine the cornstarch and cold water; add to the other ingredients and cook for 1 minute to thicken (the consistency is similar to a Chinese sweet and sour sauce).

Serve over white or brown rice. Garnish with the pineapple chunks.

CLEAN BOILED CHICKEN

This sounds really basic, but it's a very healthy way to prepare chicken. All the fat boils off and you're left with a juicy and delicious dish, one that you can serve with any number of traditional Chinese sauces: hot mustard, red chili, soy sauce or oyster sauce. You can buy the sauces pre-made in an Asian grocery store. Or you can even eat this chicken plain—it's that good!

INGREDIENTS

1 whole chicken
5–6 dried tangerine or orange peels
6 green onions
2 tablespoons sesame oil
1 clove garlic, mashed
Optional sauces: Chinese mustard,
  red chili sauce, soy sauce or
  oyster sauce; or 1 recipe Sweet and
  Sour Sauce (page 138)

Wash and clean the chicken—or let your butcher do the work for you. Cook with the skin on (this keeps the chicken juicy) and remove the skin before serving. Place the chicken breast-side down in a large pot of boiling water. Add the tangerine or orange peels for flavor. Return to a rolling boil (let it boil a second time) and then reduce the heat and simmer for 25 minutes. Then turn the chicken over and simmer again for 25 minutes.

While chicken is simmering: slice the green onions thinly and set aside. Heat the sesame oil and garlic in a shallow saucepan. After the chicken is cooked, remove the skin and arrange the meat on a platter. Top the chicken with the green onions and pour hot oil over the onions to make them sizzle. Serve with Chinese dipping sauces on the side; snow peas and brown rice round out the meal.

THE BESTA PASTA

Pasta is the staple food of a healthy lifestyle. Every elite athlete enjoys a bowl of pasta before the big game; it's also a great pre-workout meal for long-lasting energy. Complex carbs like pasta, rice and other grains will fuel your workouts better than a candy bar or other simple sugars that blow through your system like a hurricane, leaving you tired and drawn later in the day.

This particular recipe is simple and healthy—nothing fatty or creamy to mess with your cardiovascular system. Stick with the red sauces and skip the sausage and meatballs. Turkey is a great pinch hitter for fat-laden meats.

INGREDIENTS

½ onion, chopped
½ teaspoon vegetable oil
1 pound ground turkey
1 teaspoon pepper
1 teaspoon Mrs. Dash no-salt seasoning
 (you can find this in most well-stocked grocery stores)
1 jar low-fat marinara sauce
1 box rigatoni (or any other pasta)

Brown the chopped onion in the vegetable oil in a heavy pan. Add the turkey and brown. Season with pepper and Mrs. Dash. Simmer for 15 to 20 minutes, then add the marinara sauce and let simmer again for 15 to 20 minutes. Cook the pasta according to the directions on the package. Top with the sauce, serve with Garlic Bread (see recipe, page 138) and enjoy.

LOW-FAT HAWAIIAN EGG NOG

Melikalikimaka means Merry Christmas in native Hawaiian. I really love to drink egg nog at Christmas, but it's extremely high in fat. So I devised this low-fat version with nonfat milk and Egg Beaters. Egg whites replace the egg yolks for a creamier texture and lighter taste. It's still delicious; a special Hawaiian holiday treat.

INGREDIENTS

4 cups nonfat milk
1 cup Egg Beaters
2½ tablespoons sugar

2–3 teaspoons rum extract
2 egg whites
1 teaspoon nutmeg

Combine the milk, Egg Beaters, about half the sugar and rum extract in a bowl. Beat with an electric mixer until smooth. Chill. Beat the egg whites with the remaining sugar and fold into the milk mixture—the egg whites serve as a meringue. Sprinkle nutmeg over the top and serve.

SWEET AND SOUR SAUCE

A Chinese/Hawaiian sauce that I like to put on broiled chicken or fish. You can use it on the Plain Boiled Chicken dish I mentioned earlier, or just brush it onto skinless chicken breasts before grilling or broiling. It's very low in fat and calories. It has less oil than the sweet and sour sauce you'd get in a Chinese restaurant.

My mom came up with this recipe. I used to bug her about serving foods that were fattening, so she responded by adding more vinegar to the sauce in place of the oil; sugar, water and ketchup will allow the sauce to thicken without using as much oil. Sugar (in moderation, of course) makes a better base than oil because the goal is to cut down on the fat-based calories in your diet.

INGREDIENTS

½ cup vinegar
½ cup sugar
1 tablespoon cornstarch
1 cup water
2 tablespoons vegetable or canola oil
1 clove garlic, minced
¼ cup ketchup

Combine all the ingredients in a saucepan, stir and bring to a boil. Stir and simmer until thick. Makes 1½ cups.

GARLIC BREAD

Ideal with pasta—or with anything, really. This is much healthier than the usual drenched-with-butter garlic bread. And, trust me, you won't miss all that unwanted fat.

INGREDIENTS

4 slices fresh sourdough bread
½ teaspoon margarine—just enough to allow the garlic powder and the Parmesan to stick to the bread
Garlic powder, to taste—don't confuse this with garlic salt!
Parmesan cheese, to taste—don't get carried away with the cheese, please

Spread the bread lightly with the margarine and sprinkle the garlic powder and Parmesan cheese on top. Toast in a toaster oven or broiler for 3 to 4 minutes. Serve hot.

BLUEBERRY-ORANGE MAUI MUFFINS

An alternative to the standard bran muffin. I add fruit to the bran for a moister muffin. Fresh or frozen blueberries and grated orange peel (or fresh orange slices) make a world of difference. Egg whites, as usual, replace whole eggs to cut down on the fat content without diluting the flavor of the muffin, and nonfat milk replaces whole milk.

INGREDIENTS

⅓ cup oat bran
1 cup flour
1 cup oats
½ cup brown sugar
1 tablespoon baking powder
½ teaspoon salt
½ teaspoon cinnamon,
   or to taste

1 cup nonfat milk
2 egg whites, beaten
3 tablespoons oil
1 cup fresh blueberries
1 tablespoons grated
   orange peel
½ teaspoon vanilla

Preheat the oven to 425 degrees. Combine the oat bran, flour, oats, brown sugar, baking powder, salt and cinnamon in a bowl. Mix. Add the milk, egg whites and oil. Stir until moist. Fold in the fruits and vanilla.

Spray a muffin tin with nonstick spray and fill cups two-thirds full. Bake for 25 minutes. Makes nine muffins.

TROPICAL FRUIT GRANOLA DELITE

Another easy-to-prepare dessert or breakfast treat. You can't go wrong with fresh fruit, granola and yogurt. I like to eat this before a morning workout for a burst of quick energy.

INGREDIENTS

2 cups low-fat or nonfat granola
1 carton flavored nonfat yogurt
½ cup fresh bananas, strawberries or
   blueberries

Pour the granola into a cereal bowl. Add the yogurt and stir. Top with fresh fruit.

CHINESE MEATLOAF

You won't find this one on the menu at your local diner or coffee shop. Water chestnuts, egg whites, lean turkey and extra-lean ground beef transforms ordinary meatloaf into an exotic, low-fat dinner option.

INGREDIENTS

½ onion, chopped
1 pound lean ground turkey
1 pound extra-lean ground beef
2 slices bread, cubed
2 egg whites
¼ cup nonfat milk
1 teaspoon pepper
1 teaspoon sea salt
¼ cup diced water chestnuts
1 bunch cilantro, stemmed and chopped

Preheat the oven to 375 degrees. Mix the onion, turkey and ground beef in a large bowl. Add the bread, egg whites, milk and salt and pepper. Mix well. Fold in the water chestnuts, then the cilantro. Place the mixture in an oven-safe casserole dish or bowl. Bake for 40 minutes, until brown on top. Serve with white rice and your favorite vegetable.

HAWAIIAN HONEY-MUSTARD CHICKEN

Another variation on a familiar theme from my grandmother's Hawaiian kitchen on Maui. Always use skinless chicken; the pineapple juice adds moisture and tenderizes the chicken; the honey-mustard sauce is low in fat and rich in flavor.

INGREDIENTS

1 large can sliced pineapple, packed in its own juice, not in syrup—substitute fresh pineapple when available
4 boneless and skinless chicken breasts
Salt and pepper (to taste)
2 large cloves garlic
1 teaspoon thyme
2 teaspoons vegetable oil
1 tablespoon cornstarch
¼ cup honey
¼ cup Dijon mustard

Drain the pineapple; reserving the juice. Sprinkle the chicken with salt and pepper, then rub the meat with garlic and thyme. Heat the oil in a skillet until hot; cook the chicken in the hot oil until brown.

Combine the pineapple juice with the cornstarch. Mix the honey and mustard together, then stir into the skillet with the pan juices. Cover the skillet and simmer for 15 minutes. Stir the cornstarch mixture into the pan. Add the pineapple slices. Cook, stirring until the sauce thickens.

CANTONESE TOFU AND STEAMED RICE

The soybean cake is a terrific source of low-fat protein. Seasoning the hot oil first with garlic will seal in natural flavors and minimize the amount of oil that's needed to cook the tofu. Seasoning hot oil is the basis for all good Chinese cooking.

INGREDIENTS

1 tablespoon sesame oil
1 clove garlic, mashed
1 package tofu, drained
1 zucchini, sliced
1 bunch cilantro, stemmed
   and chopped

1 tablespoon low-sodium soy
   sauce, combined with 1
   tablespoon water
2 teaspoons sesame seeds
   (optional)
Cilantro for garnish (optional)

Heat a wok or deep frying pan on medium-high. Add the oil. The oil must be heated until it's very hot; if the oil is not hot enough, the tofu will simply absorb the oil. That's not what you want—very hot oil acts to seal in the natural juices of the soybean cake, rather than infuse it with the flavor of the oil.

When the oil is hot, add the garlic and stir. Add the tofu and quickly stir-fry. After 2 to 3 minutes, add the zucchini and stir-fry again. When the tofu and zucchini are cooked, reduce the heat to simmer. Add the cilantro and soy sauce/water mixture. Simmer for 2 to 3 minutes. Serve over steamed white rice; garnish with sesame seeds and cilantro if you like.

HAWAIIAN TAPIOCA PUDDING

One of my favorite desserts—I used to eat this when I was a little girl. It's just tapioca with toasted sesame seeds. Low in fat, with no oil, this is a sweet and healthy dessert that's quick and easy to make.

INGREDIENTS

½ pound brown sugar
2½ cups water
1 box (8 ounces) instant tapioca pudding
1 teaspoon sesame seeds

Boil the brown sugar in the water for five minutes. Cool.

Add the tapioca and let it sit for 15 to 30 minutes. Stir and pour into a greased 9-inch pan. Steam over high heat for 35 minutes. Sprinkle sesame seeds over the top. Cool, slice in diamond shapes and serve.

STEAMED CHICKEN AND BROCCOLI

This is a special microwave dish. You won't believe how good this tastes and how quick it is to prepare. It's very low in fat—I wouldn't have it any other way.

INGREDIENTS

½ pound skinless chicken breast
Dash of pepper

1 teaspoon water
1 stalk fresh broccoli

Rinse and dry the chicken. Slice it into pieces 1 inch thick; any length is fine. Season with pepper. Place the chicken in a microwave-safe dish, add the water and cook on high for 5 to 6 minutes. Be sure to check the chicken at 1-minute intervals until it's fully cooked.

Rinse and chop the broccoli. Place it in a plastic bag, and poke holes in the bag to allow steam to escape. Microwave on high for 5 to 6 minutes, until it's slightly crunchy. Serve the chicken and broccoli together—the whole meal takes only 15 minutes to prepare.

TIKI TUNA SALAD

A variation on Kimo's Albacore Tuna (page 145). A great summer lunch or dinner—light and yet high enough in protein to help you build and repair muscle tissue after a tough workout.

INGREDIENTS

1 large can tuna packed in spring water, drained and rinsed
½ cup plain nonfat yogurt
½ cup sliced celery

½ cup sliced green onion
4 medium tomatoes
½ cup oats
Lettuce leaves

Flake the tuna, and combine with the yogurt, celery and onion. Chill. Hollow out the tomatoes with a spoon or a knife. Stir the oats into the tuna mixture and spoon into the tomato shells. Serve on lettuce leaves. Serves four.

KIMO'S ALBACORE TUNA

I got very tired of eating plain tuna right out of the can. Yuck! Not a pretty sight, believe me. I decided to nip this plain-tuna boredom in the bud by whipping up my own tuna creation. Nonfat yogurt replaces the mayo. Carrots, cucumbers and sprouts add texture. I know it sounds strange, but I think this is the best low-fat tuna recipe you'll ever find.

INGREDIENTS

1 large can albacore tuna, drained and rinsed—
  rinsing removes excess sodium
1 large carrot
½ cucumber
½ cup plain nonfat yogurt
½ teaspoon Dijon mustard
5–6 small mandarin oranges, cut in half
Chopped almonds (to taste)
Sprouts (to taste)
Mustard (to taste)
Tomatoes, sliced (to taste)

Flake the tuna in a medium-sized bowl. Finely grate the carrot and cucumber and fold into the tuna. Combine the nonfat yogurt with the mustard and stir into the tuna. Fold in the mandarin oranges and almonds. Serve on nine-grain bread with sprouts, mustard and sliced tomatoes.

LOW-FAT YOGURT PIE

A delicious dessert that I whipped up for some friends one night at the last minute. Everyone enjoyed it so much that I decided to share it with you. It's low in fat and calories, rich in flavor and texture.

INGREDIENTS

1 large container plain nonfat yogurt
2 containers strawberry nonfat yogurt
1 small carton lite Cool Whip topping

1 package fresh or frozen strawberries, reserving some for garnish
1 graham cracker pie crust

Mix all of the yogurt and Cool Whip topping together in a mixing bowl. Fold in the strawberries. Pour the mixture into a pre-made graham cracker pie crust. Top with extra strawberries. Place in the freezer until completely frozen. Slice like a pie and serve cold.